THE LIES WE LIVE WITH

Outside the Gate

DEREK RODGERS

Copyright 2016

Outside the Gate Publishing: Copyright 2016

Published in the United States by Outside the Gate.

Richmond, VA

Printed in the United States

LOGO by: shutterstock

*DEDICATION:*

*My wife, Kristie, who was essential in my transformation. I never would have made the necessary changes without her patience and compassion.*

*Dedicated to every man and woman who attempted to guide me in the correct direction. To all the people who saw something good within me when I wanted to hide and ignore it. This is dedicated to the people who don't give up on teenagers who attempt to self-destruct.*

*It is a challenge to rise up in this world. We sometimes hide our light.*

*Thank you to those who supported me and my family... I have begun volunteering in places that nurture broken children. They need our support and patience.*

Outside the Gate Publishing

OTG Publishing is designed to educate men and women.

OTG was formed to enlighten those who know that there is

more to life than avoiding prison.

Freedom is more than self-expression and individuality.

A person can be free from prison and poverty but still

remain in bondage.

Contact:

OTG Publishing

Outsidethegate1.com

Davarim1@gmail.com

## THE LIES WE LIVE WITH

*A speaker of Truth has no friends.  -   African proverb*

**Deuteronomy 32:4**

**He is the Rock, His work is perfect; For all His ways are justice, A God of truth and without injustice; Righteous and upright is He.**

**Psalm 25:5**

**Lead me in Your truth and teach me, For You are the God of my salvation; On You I wait all the day.**

*What is truth?*

*Deuteronomy 32:4*

*He is the Rock, His work is perfect; For all His ways are justice, A God of truth and without injustice; Righteous and upright is He.*

*Psalm 25:5*

*Lead me in Your truth and teach me, For You are the God of my salvation; On You I wait all the day.*

*Psalm 25:10*

*All the paths of the Lord are mercy and truth, To such as keep His covenant and His testimonies.*

*Psalm 85:11*

*Truth shall spring out of the earth, And righteousness shall look down from heaven.*

*Psalm 86:11*

*Teach me Your way, O Lord; I will walk in Your truth; Unite my heart to fear Your name.*

*Psalm 96:13*

*For He is coming, for He is coming to judge the earth. He shall judge the world with righteousness, And the peoples with His truth.*

*Psalm 100:5*

*For the Lord is good; His mercy is everlasting, And His truth endures to all generations.*

*Psalm 119:142*

*Your righteousness is an everlasting righteousness, And Your law is truth.*

*Psalm 119:160*

*The entirety of Your word is truth, And every one of Your righteous judgments endures forever.*

*Proverbs 3:3*

*Let not mercy and truth forsake you; Bind them around your neck, Write them on the tablet of your heart,*

God's Word is the Truth

### *Introduction*

This is my second book. I am continuing to share the ideas that plague the minds of many young men and young women. I write especially for the Black men. We are at war. We live with wrong ideas and surround ourselves with the wrong people. We have enemies, but they the ones we call our friends. We are plagued by the evil media and the propaganda it shares. The entire population of America is immersed in media propaganda. Every day and night: men, women, and children are saturated with images, mottos, music, symbols, and propaganda. All of these forms of media alter the minds of children. The heavy influence the media has on the mind affects the behavior of the masses. If everyone is wrong, then the one who is right appears out of order.

Without proper guidance and supervision, the false ideas children learn will produce a belief window that affects every decision he or she makes. This book is not intended to be a compilation of excuses. Nor is this book intended to appease the conscience of the guilty. This book is intended to identify the roots of negative thinking. This material is here to highlight internal conflicts that may not have been recognized before.

This book is also personal. I had several lies implanted in my mind that ruined many years of my life. I wish I addressed them at an earlier age. Many years of pain and hardship could have been avoided. I hurt a lot of people and I was hurt by a lot of people. Hurt people hurt people. Only God Himself knows what could have been. I wish I could find the single answer to our failures. Is there an easy answer?

Thousands of Black men who grew up in my hometown of Newport News, VA became prosperous and successful in their personal lives. These men overcame the temptations and traps that were set before us. How did I fall? How did any of us fall?

Is there a valid excuse for a teenager to grow into a career criminal? Is there a valid excuse for a superior athlete to end his career acting like a street thug? Is Newport News cursed? Is any other city or town cursed? I want to know. I believe we all should search for these answers. How does two boys, with similar situations, develop into two completely different men? What was the defining factor?

This material will provide insight for Black, White, and Spanish men and women. I write for the Black men because I am Black. My two sons are both Black. I want to share from my own world view. I can only speak clearly through my belief window. If I attempt to understand the mind of a White man; I will be speculating. I don't know how a White boy feels when he sees Eminem adopt the mannerisms of a Black boy. I cannot speak from the mind of a Spanish boy in America. I do not know how he feels when all of his brothers and uncles belong to MS-13 or the

Surenos; and he does not want to join. But he has no choice. I can only speculate.

My speculation is based on knowledge and experience though. I was incarcerated with White and Spanish men. I was involved with a many White and Spanish men when I lived in Newport News and Atlanta. These men told me about their personal situations and their motivation for living a life of crime. This book is not a guessing game.

I did not want to write a book about speculation. Our schools and media is overloaded with speculation. Young people always come to me for answers. Young people want answers to their problems. Young people listen to music, watch movies, and read books for answers. They want someone to shine light in their dark worlds. People need answers, people search for answers. These kids are not addicted to media for nothing. I pray I can provide some answers. This is not a Black man's book, but it is from a Black man's mind and heart.

I pray that others may see some light after reading this book. I hope the reader will identify strongholds in his or hers own mind. It is imperative that a man or woman recognize his or hers own internal conflict. You must see the truth about yourself. We all have the ability to lie to others. We all have the capability to lie to ourselves. We do it every day. But in order to change, we must tell the truth about ourselves. Who are you? What are you living for? What is your motivation? What do you think, feel, believe, and know?

What is your truth? What is your conflict? What lie are you living with? Do you want to know the truth? Can you continue to live with the lie even after the truth has been revealed to you? What do you understand? Think about it.

***Jesus is Lord***

## COGNITIVE DISSONANCE

Before I begin to write about the concept of living with lies, I will provide a medical explanation for this condition. Science is becoming a major factor in all of the decision making of government agencies. Science is also a major factor in the decision making of public schools. The implementation of science in decision making is labeled "evidence based practices."

We all must pay attention to the medical and scientific definitions of our conditions. I am a man of faith; but I must live in this world and know how others view my condition. We all must know how to define our situations and know how others define us. Science and psychology books do not contain the word Sin. Ninety percent of science and psychology books do not incorporate God. We must know how professional institutions view us and our children.

The American Psychological Association plays a major role in our lives. The APA plays a major role in the lives of our children and loved ones. We must know what they think of people who are delusional, depressed, overstimulated, lazy, confused, and angry. We must know why the APA prescribes tons of medications to solve mental and emotional disorders. We are not required to agree with the APA and its methods. But we must know what the enemy is doing. All psychologists are not right. A title does not make a person correct in his or hers thinking. A medical degree does prove that a man or woman is using correct methods to treat clients. A degree only proves that a person can follow instructions from an exclusive institution.

I researched cognitive dissonance after hearing a lecture by Dr. Joy de Gruy Leary. She discussed the emotional and mental turmoil that surfaces from the guilt associated with misbehavior. Psychologists have a medical term used to define a person who is living with a lie.

Cognitive dissonance is the term used to describe a person who is living with a lie. Dissonance is the discomfort that exists from accepting an idea, item, or substance that a person knows is wrong. This term was first used in 1957 by a psychologist named Leon Festinger.

Festinger developed his theory of cognitive dissonance after studying social relationships that were based on rumors and lies. He discovered that people will change their minds to fit in a crowd. Festinger discovered that people will override their own conscience by adopting the mentality of their neighbors. His studies showed how people will adjust their beliefs for a role in a society, even if the new idea is wrong. How many people do you know have changed their faith, behavior, image, and speech for an idea? Even if the idea was false. How many people you know transition their lives for a role or position, even if the role or position violates their conscience? Have you ever done that? Why?

Cognitive dissonance is an internal conflict that arises from holding two incompatible thoughts in the mind at the same time. The mind must balance two opposing ideas at the same time. I know this is right, but I think it is wrong. I know this is wrong, but I think it is right.

Cognitive dissonance has several symptoms that alter the behavior of the one who is suffering from the condition. One of the symptoms is guilt. Another symptom is a severe adjustment to social circles. The person will change all of his or hers friends. Another symptom is hypocrisy. The person will say one thing and do another. Another symptom is the withholding of a lot of secrets. Many other symptoms of dissonance can be identified within the sufferer. These symptoms involve behaviors and speech. Emotional instability will also be present with the one who suffers from cognitive dissonance.

Men and women are not designed to be fake. Men and women are not designed to live with falsehood. God did not create man to exist in a constant state of malfunction. Extreme measures must be taken to override the conscience.

The mind must be altered to function in an unhealthy condition. A new mind must be created within an individual to accept a life of corruption.

The level of dissonance a man or woman exhibits is based on the person's need. The level is based on how the new idea disturbs his or hers life. I will write about this in detail in later chapters. But just consider your own life. How does your wrong ideas effect you? How do you know what ideas you live with are wrong? What lies are you living with?

How deep does dissonance exist? How many levels can a person fall into dissonance? This is a scary question. It depends on how important the idea is to the person. A good example is cigarette smoking. Why do people smoke; if they know it will kill them? Why do men and women drink and drive? Why do doctors prescribe medicine they know will kill the patient? Why do school teachers accept jobs that do not allow them to teach? How do people go to church every week and not learn anything spiritual? How can a person live as a homosexual and expect others to view it as normal? These are examples of cognitive dissonance; on different levels.

The more I study cognitive dissonance, the more I realize I can write an entire book on this subject alone. I can write about that singular subject later. I will continue to write about life outside the gate. I will write about how this condition affects our lives in the spiritual prison. Living with lies affects us spiritually, physically, and mentally. Living with lies affects our existence inside and outside of the physical prison or jail. Some lies we may not recognize. Some lies we do recognize. Other lies we attempt to hide.

Hiding internal conflict is almost impossible. Your spirit knows right from wrong. Internal conflicts impact emotions, decisions, and interpersonal relationships without our conscious permission. Dissonance is that internal instability that results from the wrestling within the mind.

Some may view cognitive dissonance as guilt or demonic influence. That is okay with me. I am not writing about those similarities or differences. I am a Hebrew. We view things with simplicity. We don't argue over labels that split hairs. The discomfort that arises because of the mind wrestling with opposing information must be identified and resolved. This issue must be addressed.

I want others to be free. I want to be free. I write about what impacts me and my loved ones. My wife and I both had to heal our minds from wrong thinking.

Is there anything good about cognitive dissonance? Yes. The discomfort proves that God gave us all a conscience. The discomfort proves that there is a difference between right and wrong. The guilt proves that something inside of us knows when we hear good or bad information. You can just feel injustice, lies, deceit, and bias in speech. I can look at a picture and almost know what the subject in the picture is feeling or thinking. I can listen to someone on television speak; and know if he or she is telling the truth. We all have a soul. Our soul knows what is acceptable and unacceptable.

The person who chooses to override the soul must now surround his or herself with others who choose to override their conscience. This can happen in gangs, government, institutions, or sports. The old phrase, "you are who you hang with!" is very true.

I will leave this topic here. Some of these concepts will be mentioned again in this writing. I just wanted to share the accepted mainstream version of living with lies. Scientists and psychologists attempt to explain human phenomena without the soul. Some of the highly educated professionals want to live in a world without guilt or God. They have their theories of human nature explain behavior without factoring in the soul.

I will write about the soul. We have a spirit within us that will not separate itself from the presence of God. Jesus said he will never let his children go away from him. Man must develop his own methods of separating himself from God. Unfortunately, we do. But we must lie to ourselves and each other to do it.

**Jesus is Lord**

## *THE LIES WE LIVE WITH*

The lies we live with. The lies we live with are responsible for so many of our social ills. Our lies paralyze us with insecurity. Our lies paralyze us with fear. The lies we live with provide a belief window that controls our behavior. The lies we live with surround us with other people who choose to accept the same lie.

Most men make decisions based upon their personal belief system. A few men live their lives through their emotions. The men who live what they believe are the ones who live by faith. That faith was provided by an external source. Some faith is good. Some faith is bad. The bad faith is the lies we accept as truths. What lies are you living with?

I ask myself several questions every day. The questions that I ask myself involve my own beliefs. I want to be assured that I am on the correct path. I want to be sure that I am not leading my wife and children into self-destruction. The man is the leader within his house. He must be on a pathway to perfection. The man must maintain a whole mind, healthy body, and clean spirit. A man's words must be wise and truthful. A man cannot live with lies.

The questions that I ask myself are about life and purpose. I ask myself, "What am I working for? I ask myself, "What am I living for?" I ask myself, "What will I do with my life today?" I have dozens of questions that I use to remind myself of my purpose. These are the questions that I offer up to the Lord Jesus Christ as prayers. I need to know that he is ordering my life. The most important question that I ask myself is, "Do I really know God?"

I believe that one of the biggest regrets a man will have when he reviews his life is when he realizes that he was wrong and did not know it. When a man realizes that he was wrong about an idea or event in his past, he may become bitter. That bitterness is the result of knowing that he cannot change his past. That bitterness is also the result of ignoring his conscience. Bitterness is a poisonous emotion. We must not ignore our conscience.

There were many seasons in my life that I ignored my conscience. I would frustrate my soul and heart by not taking heed to the prompts. Many times we know our actions are wrong. Many times we know our behavior is out of order. But we choose to believe our deeds are proper and necessary. The excuse is always the same. The excuse is usually, "someone told me to do that." Another common excuse is, "I just was not thinking at the time." A popular excuse for bad behavior is, "Everybody else is doing it." peer pressure is very real and very influential. If a man surrounds himself with people who all believe the same lie; it will become the truth. It is only the truth to that group. Surrounding yourself with people who all believe the same lie is also a method of ignoring your conscience.

When I was young and stupid, I would use many excuses for negative behaviors. I would live like every day could be my last. I wanted to have some fun and excitement to feel alive. I used to think that I was missing something. I subconsciously accepted the lie that tomorrow does not matter as long as today was full. Most of this wrong thinking is the result of depression. A man self-destructs when he no longer chooses to follow truth. The lies will lead him away from his True and Living God.

The depression I experienced was the result of accepting lies. I did not have the vision, purpose, plan, or proper goals for my life. This lack of direction left me vulnerable to evil and other misguided men. Most of us lacked vision and proper leadership. We were blind men leading other blind men. A lost man will accept a lie because it is a new idea. He will not accept the lie because it is correct. But he will accept the lie because it produces a new adventure. We must not accept any information that is not true. The adventure may be short but the impact of the adventure can damage a life for years.

An example of a lie that leads men on adventures is the myth of the Player. A teenager will fantasize about being a player. I wanted to be a ladies man for years. This adventure is fun for a limited amount of time. But the damage caused by dating and sleeping with hundreds of women cannot be reversed. AIDS and other sexually transmitted diseases ruined the lives of millions of adults. Millions of children have also suffered because of this immoral sexual behavior. God never designed the Player. The imagination of sensuous, perverted men produced this character.

Life is an adventure. We were intended to explore the earth and explore possible relationships with each other. We were also expected to invent new ideas, structures, and technologies. I also realized that we were supposed to explore one another. Every man, woman, and child contains different ideas and different inspiration. We form our identities based on our interactions with other people. It is extremely important that our identities are built on truths and not falsehoods. Our adventures must be journeys in the light. When we live in falsehood, our adventures are journeys in the dark.

This writing is intended to identify the lies we live with that have created an existence that is absolutely wrong. I believe we have generated a world that is completely out of order. The result is a high rate of suicide, crime, and mental illness. Men and women are attempting to fit into a world that is unfit for survival. We distract ourselves from the chaos with sports, musical events, and religion. But the truth is that we are finding our positions in a system that must be corrected.

The error in our thinking is the fact that we compromise to fit into this world's system. This error must be corrected. We must stop altering our character and modifying our thinking to fit into a corrupt world. Instead, we must analyze the world. We must recognize the darkness of the world. How can we teach a child to fit into a corrupt world without corrupting the child? When we purify ourselves, we can shift the mindset of the culture. A clean mind can receive the truth. A clean and pure man will expose the lies.

The culture we live in must be fixed. Young men and young women are confused by the way the world operates. These young people are choosing to self-destruct instead of existing in a world they see as faulty. I talk to teenagers who see no hope for the future. This lack of hope causes many of them to choose a life of crime and fantasy. It becomes a waste of time attempting to teach these young people to integrate into a world that they hate.

The young ones have a view of the world that prevents them from being submissive. Rebellion is their mentality of choice. I went through that same rebellious stage. We must attempt to change the culture. We cannot expect people to endorse a world that is wicked. If we assimilate into a wicked world, we will only create more wicked men.

If everyone believes the lie, the one who does not accept the lie is viewed as an outcast. This fear of expulsion will cause a child to accept the lie to fit into the community. When this lie is passed from one generation to another, it becomes a tradition. Traditions never end. A tradition must die out with the ones who accept it.

Outcasts are not the majority. The outcasts are the minority. The majority are usually the ones who are wrong in their thinking. The majority maintains its stronghold over the culture by excluding anyone who enters with the truth. The crucifixion of Jesus Christ is the proof of that behavior. The people who have their faith in the death, burial, and resurrection of Jesus Christ are excluded from lodges, institutions, and exclusive government positions.

The falsehoods we live with prevent us from accepting those who attempt to prove us wrong. I always wondered why I hated people who lived with joy. I always wondered why some of my friends would become resentful when I talked about self-improvement. Most of them did not want to do better.

The irony is how I avoided the topics involving Jesus Christ but I entered the conversations about Buddha, Allah, Malcolm X, and Marcus Garvey. I would only avoid Jesus. The truth is that Jesus changes his disciples. The other religions allow men to change themselves. Do you really want to be transformed? Or do you want to change just enough to find a position in the current culture? If you are transformed, God will not allow you to fit into the current culture.

The falsehoods that immerse our world appear in many aspects of our lives. We hear half-truths from the media, music, and social commentators. We are indoctrinated by family lies masquerading as traditions. There are times we accept a curse or negative opinion offered by a parent. Dishonesty is one of the first lessons a child learns. We feel violated the first time we are lied to by a friend or a loved one. We feel violated the first time our father or mother does not fulfill a promise. I reached a point in my life where I believed everyone is lying. I remember not wearing a watch because I didn't believe the time.

A lot of Black men are sick. But who is there to heal us? Nobody.

A few other lies that shape our thinking involve street myths, character impersonations, Hollywood lies, propaganda, mis-education, and emotional falsehood. The street lies are the slang terms and language we use to convey ideas. Even though our words have no meaning. We learn exaggerations and superstitions from these concepts.

Most men and women have the wrong definition of love. Love is not an emotion that dictates our actions. Love is a decision. Love is a power that binds. Love does not free a person. Love binds a person.

Because I love my wife, I am bound to her. I am commited to my wife. I will not abandon her. Love is a power that binds. I love my wife so I will not share my body with another woman. Love is not a freedom, it is a bonding. Love makes a person sacred. Love does not remove boundaries. Love builds boundaries.

The other misrepresentation we adopt is about God. What is God? Who is God? These questions must be asked and answered. We form false religions and strange traditions with our imperfect views of God.

This book will explore the many falsehoods we all share. Our culture in America appears to be based on many falsehoods. The children who search for truth are compelled to end their investigations. The search separates the person who embarked on the search from his or hers peers. The separation produces anxiety and isolation. I will write about how I was discouraged from learning truth. I will also attempt to explain how we live in a world laced with lies and now many of us do not recognize the lies because we learned to exist by them. The truth is now uncomfortable. We have been wrong for so long, we have trouble living right.

The Creator designed men to be able to adapt to any type of existence that he desires. We can live wickedly and be satisfied with our lives. It is possible to guide your own path to hell. Or, you can live a righteous life and be satisfied with the way God guides your life. Jesus said I am the Way, the Truth, and the Life. There is no life without him. He is the way. He is the Truth. Anything other than Jesus is not Truth. What lies are you living with?

The lies we live with exist in many different forms. I will mention some of them in this book. I can never identify every falsehood in our lives. Too many aspects of our lives are based on lies. Each lie leads to another lie. Each of us must uncover the original lie. Then we can restore our true nature. The soul at peace is the soul that is living in truth.

## THE FIRST LIE

What is the first lie you ever told someone? Do you remember? What was the first lie that someone else spoke to you? Do you remember? I do not remember the very first lie I heard. I do not remember the first lie I told. The first lie introduced us all to a world of deception we never should have experienced. The Bible said we are born into a dying world.

I do not remember the first introduction I received of deception. I do remember the trauma I felt, early in life, from being hurt and disappointed by people I trust. I can remember the feeling of being disappointed by my parents. I can remember when they said they would do something and then not do it. I can remember when teachers said they would do something and not do it. As a child, we do not understand the difference between a lie and an error in judgment. We just hear an adult say, "I will" or "Yes." And the adult does not fulfill his or hers promise. These moments produce disillusionment and frustration. I learned a lesson I should not have learned. I learned that I can say one thing, and do another thing without any consequence.

Children learn how to lie early in life. Children witness adults telling lies when they are young. When an adult lies and does not repent of that lie; he or she is being a negative example to a child. The child will model that same behavior and tell lies fearlessly: believing that no consequence is attached to that lie. The lies we live with do come with consequences. The sad truth is that we do not understand the weight of these consequences until we create a life for ourselves that is unbearable.

The first lie is an important moment in a child's life. The first lie can continue to harm a person into his or hers adult's life. The way a man or woman begins his thinking pattern produces a permanent character. That character develops a personal belief system. That personal belief system cultivates a certain pattern of behavior.

These moments of evolution are the foundation of a person's life. The child becomes an adult. The adult is the product of the child. A child who is built by truth will grow into an adult assembled by truth. A child who is built by deception will grow into an adult assembled by deception.

The first lie must be identified. What was the first lie that was imparted to you? Can you identify the lie that formed your pattern of thinking? How can that lie be identified? What will you do when you recognize the lie?

One of the first lies I entertained was in a movie. The movie was *Conan the Barbarian*. I witnessed several actors being killed by swords and knives. I was a young boy. I was seven or eight years old. When I was watching this movie; I felt uncomfortable seeing these actors die. I still remember the conversation I had with the other boy in the room. He said, "That is not real. The men in the movie are only acting like they are dead." Then he said, "They get paid to die. It is not real." That moment changed my whole world view. You can act like somebody you are not and benefit from it.

At the time, I did not realize what was happening to my mind. I did not realize that I would learn to never believe what I see with my own eyes. I was being indoctrinated into a way of thinking. I started to learn not to believe what I saw with my own eyes. I started to doubt the things that I witnessed. The curse of television is that we see images that are not real. These false images produce a life of insecurity and doubt. My mind became a mind filled with doubt and insecurity. I began to not believe what I was told. I began to doubt everything I heard and saw.

This incident alone did not damage my conscience. This incident alone did not lead me on a path of confusion. I was also witnessing dishonesty in other forms. I had classmates in school who lied about assignments and behavior. The lies were so plain but they benefited from them. Also noticed how certain people got away with offering their false statements. Another student could tell the same story and be punished for it. I learned how favoritism operates at an early age.

Children with an inclination to lie, cheat, or steal; should not be enabled by adults in the positions of authority. We do not need any help becoming mischievous. A child who is enabled by an adult may learn that his or hers evil behavior is not wrong. This is dangerous because he or she may never change.

My life started as a religious walk. That walk was okay as long as I was surrounded by other religious people. I had trouble translating that walk to school and the community. Once I learned that a liar can prosper, I decided to learn more about it. I eventually started lying. I just wanted to see what I can get away with. We all have a Genesis Chapter 3 moment. The moment when wrong is not wrong. The moment when the rules appear to be a roadblock to freedom. The liar creates his own world. A world where only the ones who accept the lie can enter. The liar becomes a God of this illegitimate world. The liar is an antichrist. The foundation for wickedness was being erected.

The ability to lie and not be punished for it is attractive to children because it allows them to craft an alternate reality. The power to craft and create a personal reality satisfies the human desire to be like God. If I was wise, I would never have allowed my mind to venture into darkness. Or maybe I was already dark. I just needed an instigator to reveal it.

I should have accepted the movie as entertainment and not attributed the images to the real world. My pliable mind should not have been confused by a movie. I would not blame a movie on my life of sin. I can write a dozen books on the damage Hollywood has done to the souls of children. I am just mentioning one instance in my early life that altered my world view. I learned to doubt what I see. I learned that deception can be used for entertainment. Maybe I should have been a magician.

This incident is one of the first moments that initiated my entrance into my world of deception. I began to change when I stopped believing what I could clearly see. I stopped accepting everything I witnessed in church. I stopped trusting the words authority figures spoke. I wanted to assume everyone was lying. I even discovered methods to deceive myself.

I became fascinated with illusion during this season of my life. Magic became interesting. Cheating became fun. Trickery was something I wanted to master. I also started to practice lying to girls and teachers. Whenever I was caught lying; I would just say that it was a joke. Or I would say that I was acting. The assumption that I was making is that there should be no consequences. I also operated with the assumption that no one would be hurt. Other people were consumed with living in their own world and did not hold me accountable for my fables. Many men and women are never exposed for their misdeeds. The people that surround them are also living in a façade.

I accepted many other lies as I continued to live my life. The lies I learned later were easy to accept because I was so far from the truth. The truth is Jesus Christ. I accepted lies about many aspects of the world. Some of the lies young men accept are attached to membership. I would believe a lie to belong to a group of friends. I also accepted lies because I did not want to be persecuted by others. The first lie is damaging because it can leave a child disoriented for years.

What foundation could I stand on if I do not trust what I see? What foundation could I stand on if do not trust the authorities who were placed in my life?

What was your first lie? What is your foundation? What are you willing to live for? What are you willing to die for? What do you believe? Are you willing to die for that belief? What if you learned that what you believe is a lie? Will you repent and be taught the truth? Will you accept the truth when it arrives?

I experienced this process of change. It hurt. I had to have my whole mind renewed and restored. I spent most of my life living in a fog. All because of a few simples ideas that were not true. When I first learned that these ideas were not true; I worked very hard to make them true. I could not stand the thought of admitting to myself that I wasted so many years of my life. I was willing to die to defend my lie.

The first lie in a boy or girls life is probably the most damaging one. I say that the first lie is the most damaging lie because it propels a person into deeper forms of dishonesty. A child has a clear conscience. That conscience must remain clear. The clear conscience has no trouble seeing deception. A clear conscience will refrain from accepting fraud and dishonest speech. A child must recognize deception and reject it. The child who accepts deception will enter the world of deception and learn to enjoy it.

## THE WORLD OF DECEPTION

The world of deception is just as real as the world God created. This world of deception is real because men, women, and children choose to exist inside of it. The world of deception involves images, propaganda, entertainment, distractions, physical excitement, and man-made institutions. The world of deception exists because many people work together to maintain its existence. Liars walk together to maintain the life of the lie. Human technology and human philosophy sustain lies and invite others into the fantasy. People agree to accept the lie. Just like a Masonic lodge. They all know it is wrong.

I believe we attempt to live our whole life in this world of deception. The world of deception allows men and women to become a form of God. We learn this fact as children. I can generate my own reality by repeating my ideas and then surrounding myself with other people who are willing to accept my ideas. Fraternities and sororities help sustain ideas. Churches help individual groups sustain ideas. What happens when everyone believes the same fable? It becomes the truth.

This fact is exhibited when we choose our friends. Most of our friends see the world the same way we view the world. The one who is the group leader determines how the rest of the group thinks. The followers in the group wait for approval from their friends within the group before he or she makes a personal decision.

I remember when I avoided going to college in 1997 and 1998. I could have enrolled but the people I was fellowshipping with at this time did not go to college. I was afraid to build my own path and chose not to go. I also had chances to register for the Armed Forces. Once again I talked myself out of it because I wanted to remain a part of my team.

The way we think hinders our decisions. The people we surround ourselves with create an atmosphere that affects our thoughts. I was accepting a position in the world that was not my true position. I adopted an image of myself that I should never have held. I allowed my environment and other negative stimuli change my opinion of myself. I wasted many years of my life. But that was not the true tragedy. The true tragedy is that I did not know I was wrong. I did not know I was destroying my life and hampering the lives of my future children.

As long as a person exists in the world of deception; he or she will seek comfort, amusement, temporary pleasures, and power. He or she will seek exclusive knowledge to remain inside this world. The exclusive knowledge will come from social commentators who endorse the fantasy world a person wants to live inside. Men and women who choose to live in darkness will use the media to remain in that condition. The darkness becomes normal. Music, movies, magazines, and books are available to validate any belief system an adult or child endorses.

When I thought I was a drug dealer; I listened to music that contained drug dealing lyrics. When I thought I was the new Malcolm X; I watched movies about freedom fighters. When I decided to be a rebel against the mainstream; I listened to angry music and read books about revolution. I needed to remain in a state of disorder. I used the media to support my delusion.

The technology that is available to us becomes the chains that bind our minds to everything that is wrong. I see men and women who need to be freed from their mental enslavement stay trapped because all of the wrong information is ever present. Negative ideas and misconceptions about life are pressed upon their minds.

The world of deceit is easy to live in. I had everything I needed to blind myself from the truth. When I wanted to reject the Lord Jesus Christ, I could find books and pamphlets to help me feel self-righteous. I subscribed to several other religions because I wanted to find alternative meanings to life. I read books about other cultures because I wanted to redefine good and evil. I could find a television program to distract me from reality.

Movies are produced every month that provide excuses for my failures in life. The media provides all the excuses men need to justify their criminal acts. When I was incarcerated, we all had excuses. Few of us actually accepted responsibility for our actions.

Sick people cannot ask sick people for a cure. A lost man cannot ask a lost man for direction. I was in a state of depression for a season of my life. I did not recognize that state of depression. The culture we live in lacks compassion. A child should never be allowed to remain in a depressed state. Someone must be available to help lost children.

Teenagers need supervision and counsel to grow properly during the mystifying high school years. I needed help and there was no one available who committed his or herself to help me. I also had friends whose minds were just as disenchanted as I was. We attempted to help each other grow. But a fool cannot educate a fool. A blind man cannot guide a blind man to light. We needed someone with light.

I stayed in a state of depression for almost eight years. I did not know I was depressed because most of the people I was surrounded by were also in darkness. Pain and misery became normal. We learned how to avoid happy people. We assumed that the happy people were the fake and prideful ones. The truth is that the happy people were the ones who learned how to overcome the deception. The happy people were the ones who educated themselves. The truth is that the happy people were the ones who accepted their faults and perfected their gifts. I was depressed and hated happy people. I was depressed and did not know it.

Maybe I did not want to know I was depressed. Maybe I was afraid that there was a demand placed on my life. When a man accepts his faults and fortifies his talents; a demand is placed upon him. He must make a positive impact on the world. God demands it. The Bible states that no man lives for himself.

What if we intentionally remain in darkness because we do not want to serve God? I truly think that is what happened to me. It is hard to admit. What if I just refused to serve the True and Living God? What if all these Black men are killing Black men because we refuse to give our lives to God? We would rather die for our hood, die for our gang, die for money, and die for street credibility; instead of living for Jesus. The world of deception. We choose this world.

How does a man remain in the world of deception and not desire to be freed from it? We enjoy it. I satisfied my soul with sex, drugs, loud music, and pride. I also played a lot of sports and worked several challenging jobs. I knew something in my soul was dying. I channeled that misery into exciting challenges. I embarked on new challenges and created adventure. I only attached myself to adventurous people.

The adventures occupied all my time. The adventures consumed all of my energy. The world of deception does not feel like a false existence because of all the activity I was involved in. I just felt like the average man. I worked every day and found a party every night. The weekends were consumed with alcohol and weed. I would look for new clubs to attend. I stayed busy to find some fulfillment. I never knew how much it would cost me to avoid the truth. The truth is Jesus Christ. The deception is everything else.

I avoided quiet moments. I always had a book or some music in my possession. Moments of solitude caused me to feel a guilty conscience. Moments of solitude produced fear because I knew there was something else in life that I might be missing. The Creator will place ideas in men that do not come from any manmade source. Those ideas almost always contradicted what my friends and I were thinking. I believe that God himself wanted to draw me out of my own madness.

The world of deception becomes unbearable when a man or woman attempts to know the True and Living God. Jesus is the only one who can free a person from his or hers own deception. The lie we live with is: I can produce a life for myself without God.

The world of deception consists of many components. It is a complex world. Many fine pieces exist within the world of deception. I have attempted to fix this world many times. I have attempted to change that world. I wanted to use knowledge, charisma, wisdom, and even love to alter that world. It is impossible to change that world. No human can change that world. The pieces it consists of are based on falsehood.

I was constantly being deceived and setback in my own development attempting to change the dark side. Just like Luke Skywalker, when he lost his right hand, I was damaged attempting to fight darkness with my own human strength. The world of deception is too dark and consists of too many components for a man to change it. Darkness must be eradicated. A man must be removed from it.

Each component is designed to counter the original design of creation. These components can only be removed from the mind of a man by the original Creator. The original designer has to rescue a man from the dark side. A man must first recognize and realize that he is in darkness. I label this darkness deception because I did not know when I was being deceived. I just know I was stressed out all the time. But one of the first lies is that stress is essential. Without stress I am not alive, but the truth is that stress almost killed me. That stress made me want to kill others. Most of that stress could have been avoided.

Each component is crafted to alter how men and women relate to the world. Each component is designed to alter the original purpose of an item, idea, or substance. One of my first failures was losing faith in myself. I lost faith in my five senses. I could not put faith in my senses. I could not put faith in people. What could I trust but my emotions? Emotions change by the second. That is why I was so unstable.

I will attempt to explain these components. I will use my personal experiences to explain how the lies we live with alter everything we think, feel, and believe.

## HALF TRUTHS

The half-truth is a very cunning lie. The half-truth is guile. The average person cannot separate the false evidence from the true evidence. The half-truth can ruin a person's life without any detection. Many of us only focus on the information contained in an idea that appeals to our vanity or need. A half-truth will attract someone who is looking for justification of a belief system. A half-truth will also assist a liar by appeasing his or hers guilty conscience. The most seductive element of the half-truth is the fact that it looks good. A half-truth will almost always allow the listener to justify his or hers position.

An example of a half-truth would be a statement like, "It is my life; I can do what I want to do." That is a true statement. It is your life. You can do what you want to do. But the flaw in this statement is its lack of substance. This statement lacks integrity. A person will reveal his or hers heart through speech. What type of person makes this statement? What is the motive behind these words? This half-truth is fundamentally flawed.

The flaw in this statement is that a person can do whatever he or she wants to do. No one can do whatever he or she wants to do. Complete freedom is impossible. Living without rules is anarchy. If every man did what he wanted to do; our cities would be full of chaos. Your life is not your own. It is a half-truth because we do make our own decisions. But the whole truth is we make decisions within certain parameters.

The other flaw in this statement is that a person may believe, "It is my life." That is not wholly true either. We do not own ourselves. We can choose what we eat. We can choose how we dress. We can choose where we live. Sometimes we have the ability to choose our jobs. But we really do not own ourselves. That is a sad truth I had to learn. Someone else controls our lives. Even if a man does not want to admit he is subordinate to God, he is still subject to the bill collector. Many of us remain subordinate to our fathers. Everyone I know still respects the wishes of their mothers. We do not own ourselves.

We want to live like we own our lives. The truth is that we don't own ourselves. We behave like we are sovereign. We act like we are sovereign. We do not own our lives or our bodies. God owns us. When we are born; our parents are responsible for us. If you have a social security number; the U.S. government has an authority over you.

I wanted to live without rules for years. I attempted to be totally free from authority. It did not happen. I could never be free from all the rules and expectations placed on me. The culture does not permit this type of existence. I would have to be a homeless man. Even if I was a homeless man with no job to report to; I would be invading someone's private property to find rest or food. That invasion would require that I obey him or her to obtain what I need.

I could mention an extreme example of the desire for total freedom. I could live in the remote areas of the forest that are uninhabited. Build my own wooden cabin and be free from society and its responsibilities. But that is not total freedom either.

The only state of total freedom is psychosis. Psychosis is a form of mental insanity. A man would have to lose his own mind to experience total freedom.

There are rules in nature. I would have to eat something. Now I am depending on the Earth to follow the rules so I can eat. I would be subject to the weather and the animals. The first truth is that God would still be present. No one is completely free.

I was full of pride once upon a time. I manifested a strong, inflated ego once upon a time. I needed to be a unique individual to feel secure with myself. I had to be different to feel like I was in control of my life. Individuality is not wrong. It is the motive that compels the selfish character to manifest that pollutes the personality.

Individuality is a condition that causes men and women to develop unique fashions. Individuality is what leads us to adopt nicknames. Body art is another attempt to feel ownership of one's own body. "My body belongs to me." I can alter it anyway I want. The desire for uniqueness is a symptom of realizing that our lives are not ours. Deep inside we know we are not Gods. But we created a world that enables us to pretend we are Gods.

I grew dreadlocks in my hair. This was an attempt to be an individual who appeared free. I also received a few tattoos. I wanted to alter my appearance. I was not satisfied with the work God performed. My ego decided that I can do a better job of shaping my image than Him. "I can do what I want to do." "It is my life." "This is my body." A subtle change in my appearance was more than a fashion statement. It was a rebellious act.

How many rebellious acts have you performed under the guise of fashion or a trend? How did peer pressure alter your behavior? Dreadlocks are not wrong. My motive was wrong. Tattoos are wrong because the Bible said so.

Individuality is something we are taught to seek. I want to reiterate that being uniqueness is not the problem. The problem is the motive. I was seeking uniqueness because I needed to feel control. I was seeking uniqueness because I was not satisfied with the condition of my life. I knew I could do better.

A good sign that our lives are not our own is the need for employment. Why do you need a job? If we were really free to do what we want, why do men and women seek jobs? If you can do whatever you want with your life, why do you go to school? Why do we attend colleges and universities after school? This is because we are not free. This lie must be acknowledged and then rejected.

I have lost my ability to reason during several seasons of my life. I was suffering from anxiety attacks and manic depression. This was the result of wanting to believe I was free while living like a slave. I wanted to believe that I was working for myself. I wanted to believe that I was getting an education for myself. I also tried to convince myself that I was accomplishing these feats by myself. I had to appease my sense of liberty. I needed to feel independent to maintain my façade.

The breakdowns I suffered were the result of realizing I was not free. When I was challenged at work; I would rebel against my supervisors and dare them to fire me. I had to maintain my superior image. I hated to hear my co-workers say that they needed this job to keep their house. That is why I never bought a house. I did not want to be trapped. I would ridicule those men who were trapped by mortgages. When I finally had my own house, I hated it.

There is no limit to the damage a half-truth can cause. One lie will affect every decision you make in your life. One lie will alter your course by one degree. The further you travel; the further off course you will land at the end of the journey.

My nervous breakdowns were medicated with alcohol. It is ironic how I can live with the lie of liberty, but still be addicted to alcohol. Why can't I live without the liquor if I am free? We live with these lies and it becomes the new normal.

A popular fable I hear is used by most of us. This half-truth is, "I can change myself." How many different times have you said this line? "I can change myself." This is a half-truth. You can change some behaviors. A man can stop eating candy. A woman can stop overdosing on chocolate. A child can stop skipping class. Human beings do possess the ability to alter behaviors. You can change some aspects of yourself.

This idea of self-transformation is a debate that will not end until Jesus Christ returns. Men and women have invented thousands of religions that attempt to promote self-transformation. I have changed a few things in my life on my own. I stopped eating pork all by myself. I did not pray about it. I did not go on an extended fast. I did not seek a psychiatrist or doctor to assist me in my dietary adjustment. I just stopped eating pork.

This idea of changing oneself is debatable. We want to think we have invented methods of self-improvement. People hope these self-improvement methods are successful. Bookstores are stocked with books written on the subject of self-help. The Christian section in bookstores consist of self-help books. I see hundreds of self-help books in several different sections. The Buddhist section; the Hindu section; the scientific, atheist section; the student section; and the student section of the bookstores are all stocked with self-help material. Why are so many books being written by authors who believe that people can change themselves?

If men and women can change themselves, then why is the world becoming a worse place to live? If men and women can change; then why is the crime in America becoming worse? If men and women can change; why is the divorce rate so high? If men and women can change; why can't cigarette smokers quit smoking cigarettes? Humans cannot change themselves. We can only adjust a few behaviors.

The concept that a man can change himself is a half-truth. A man cannot change himself because the root cause of his decisions rest in the mind and soul. A woman cannot change herself because the source of her desires is in the mind and soul. How can a person adjust his or hers soul? You can't. That is why you must be born again.

The idea of transformation is noble. A man or woman who tries to change is wise. It is a good endeavor. The whole truth is that men and women usually stop one behavior and substitute it for another behavior. A man may stop enjoying pornography and substitute that passion with exercise. Removing the porn addiction is a positive step. But the substitution only masks the internal conflict that exists.

Substituting positive actions for negative actions is a quick fix. This quick fix allows a damaged man to hide his faults. This quick fix allows a woman to conceal her fears. But the heart of the individual still remains tainted. The healing has not occurred.

When I quit smoking cigarettes, I did not address my compulsive behavior. I substituted cigarettes for chocolate and chewing gum. I never addressed the brokenness inside me that imitated the need to smoke. I traded one bad habit for another bad habit. Chocolate is less poisonous than cigarettes but my heart was still damaged. My soul was still dark. I had no power to change myself.

I medicated my fears and depression for years. I never had a porn addiction but I did abuse alcohol. I hid that obsession by the grace of God. I never admitted I was addicted to the alcohol. I came to the realization of it after I stopped drinking. I smoked weed for almost seven years. When I stopped smoking weed, it was a little easier for me to stop drinking. When I stopped drinking, I stopped smoking.

I obviously felt better about myself after ending my substance abuse. I began exercising at a local gym. I joined American Family fitness in 2003. I channeled all of my negative energy into a new pride. I worked out seven days a week. My self-hate sent me on a mission to produce the perfect body. I achieved that goal in a year. I stopped abusing drugs and alcohol. I began abusing energy and protein substances. Same behaviors, different substances. I thought I was changing myself. I was just readjusting an ugly picture.

I never fixed what was inside me. I was whitewashing my outer appearance, but inside me were dead man bones. The new muscle and the absence of fat did not heal my heart. I cannot change myself. I can only change my behavior and my appearance. A half-truth because there are elements of oneself that a man or woman can modify. The fact is that we are a soul living in a body.

A human being is a living soul that exists inside a body. Sometimes we can change a few aspects of our way of life. Sometimes we can change our attitude. We can even change our environment and associate with different people. Regardless of these transformations; men and women need to restore his or hers soul to be whole.

The lie we live with states that an attitude adjustment is enough. If it was that easy, then why is the world filled with anger, depression, overweight adults, caffeine addicts, suicidal teens, and sexual deviants? Why?

Many other half-truths exist in our culture. Many other half-truths impact the way we view the world. The worst effect of the half-truth is the way it taints our relationships with others. The Bible discusses how men and women would create a world built on faulty human wisdom. Our answers to life's issues are never complete. We are not God.

An example of a half-truth is when a woman claims that she needs a man with money to be happy. Another half-truth is when a man says I need to have street credibility to be a real man. Women with children and no husband believe they do not need a man to raise their children. Another half-truth.

"You get what you deserve." This is a popular phrase. I have used this phrase hundreds of times. It is not a true statement. But this statement is a good concept to use as a measuring stick. If a man believes that he gets what he deserves, it will compel him to work harder. If a woman believes that she gets what she deserves, it will compel her to live with integrity.

The reason this is a half-truth is because men, women, and children are mistreated each and every day. Children are abducted each and every day. The children who are kidnapped did not deserve it. The parents who lost their children did not deserve it. I remember the story involving the women who were trapped in the basement for over a decade. Those women did not deserve that cruel treatment. I remember being convicted of a robbery I did not commit in 1995. Did I deserve that? No. None of the victims of crime and injustice deserved their punishment.

Men, women, and children are mistreated each and every day. This planet, we call Earth, is not Heaven. Bad deeds are committed against good people on a daily basis. I had friends who stole items from my car after I drove them around the city. I had a friend steal an expensive item from my house. We do not get what we deserve in this life. I wish we did. How many of us are lied to or disappointed by our friends and family?

How often have you received what you deserved? How often does your positive deeds get overlooked? How often are your mistakes magnified?

## FAMILY LIES

I have been married over 12 years. I was told by many men that marriage is not a good life. I was told by many men that marriage is not a fun, fulfilling life. The media also immerses men in the idea that marriage is the removal of a man's manhood. The analogy of a wife becoming a ball and chain is presented to us. I can only think of one good marriage that was presented on television as I grew up. That ideal, positive marriage was the *Cosby Show*. That show stopped airing on television in the early 1990's. Very few positive images are on the television this decade.

The lies about family life are infinite. I was told that I would be unhappy getting married. That is a half-truth. I was told that I would never be satisfied with one woman for the rest of my life. That was a half-truth. Many other half-truths threaten the institution of marriage. I almost avoided the idea. So many negative stories about marriage, so few positive stories about marriage. Half-truths could have changed my mind.

I married my son's mother because I did not want anyone else to marry her. I did not want anyone else to raise my son. I married my son's mother because it felt like the honorable action. I also did it to accept the challenge. I wanted to prove to myself and any critic that a man can be happy and married. I also knew that I would not be totally happy living the single life.

Single men juggle women. That is not always fun either. Juggling women can be dangerous. Juggling women also costs money, time, and enormous amounts of energy. Why not be consumed with one woman and avoid the dangers of disease and multiple pregnancies?

Happiness is possible in a marriage. A man should marry the woman who is his friend. A man should marry the woman who has the same long-term goals he has. A man should marry the woman who will support him when he needs it. That is the truth.

The reason that some men are not happy in marriage is because this world is not Heaven. No one is happy each and every day. Situations change in a family. There will be periods of stress and uncertainty. There will be moments that a man and a woman disagree. I am not on one accord with my wife seven days a week. We all must accept the fact that no relationship is perfect. No two people can be thinking the same idea or thought all the time. Expect imperfection. Make room for pain and discomfort.

Another cause of discomfort in a marriage is the enhancement stage. Men who say that they are divorced because he and the wife began hating each other is probably telling the truth. This is also only part of the truth. My wife has made me unhappy for long periods of time. I made her unhappy for long periods of time. Marriage is not designed to make both parties happy. Marriage is designed to make the man and the woman holy. Happiness and joy are the fruit of becoming holy.

The woman will expose everything that needs improvement in the man. The man will expose traits in his wife that need to be improved. All marriages will have this enhancement stage. This stage is not designed to end the marriage. This stage is purposed to make the man and the woman whole. My wife identified many parts of my character that are bad. I need to fix these aspects of my own soul and not be upset with her for pointing them out.

I believe many marriage's fail in this season because the two parties did not want to change. When the man and the woman began to expose each other; they became opponents instead of therapists.

Another half-truth is the men and women who think they do not need to be married to cultivate a family. These men and women decide to live together and never be married. This is a mistake. This is a half-truth. You do not need to be married to start a family. A man and a woman can live together and be satisfied.

The problem with this condition is the fact that there is no spiritual connection among these couples. The other problem is that there is no spiritual commitment within these couples. The purpose of marriage is for the man and the woman to commit themselves to each other before their Creator. The man and woman together commit to a covenant with God. God will then use them both to make each other perfect and fulfill the will of God through their lives. Their children will grow up under the supervision of God and their Godly parents. This family will represent God on the Earth. They become a testimony of God: and his grace and mercy. God designed every Earthly experience to bring us closer to him.

It is true that a man and a woman can have a family without marriage. It is true that the man and the woman may enjoy their lives together. I lived with my wife for almost two years before we were married. Those two years were full of extremes. Without the commitment, we both felt extremely happy and extremely afraid. We pleased each other because of the fear of losing each other. We did not serve each other through humility and love. It was a state of, "I love you as long as I get what I want."

A relationship between a man and a woman who are not married will not consist of love, commitment, compassion, and understanding. This type of relationship will consist of anxiety, passion, fear, and selfishness. These relationships are utilitarian. Utilitarian describes the using of a person, place, or thing. The person just performs a function.

I experienced all of these symptoms. The lack of commitment prevented me from making the necessary sacrifices to please my wife. Her lack of commitment led to a lack of trust and obedience. My wife knew she could pack her clothes and move back to Georgia whenever she wanted.

She was tolerating my actions for as long she wanted. Our relationship did not consist of the unconditional love written in the Bible.

We need the marriage commitment and covenant with God to establish the family he desires. Marriage is not designed to be a game of advantage. When a marriage becomes a game of advantage someone will suffer. A marriage can be miserable if it is misunderstood. A marriage can be miserable when a man or woman does not understand its proper function.

Satisfaction with one woman is a matter that I was taught is impossible by older men. I was always told that it is impossible to settle down with one woman for my entire life. That fear did affect the way I behaved as a young adult. Before I had a child, I considered the conditions that needed to be present if and when I was married. I looked for men who were satisfied with their wives. It did not happen often.

When I did meet a man who was content with his wife; he was either a religious man or a man who was subordinate to his woman. I had no desire to be religious; and I had no desire to be subordinate. I knew hundreds of married men; but very few of them were good role models. I met many men who were unfaithful to their wives. The idea that men cannot be satisfied with one woman is very compelling. I wanted to believe it.

How can a man be faithful to one woman? What is the key to remaining faithful? The answer to these questions and many more is the same. Heal the soul. We believe we need multiple women to be happy because we are not in our right minds. Why does a man need a different woman every week? He does not need a different woman every week. Being faithful requires a man to understand what is driving him to feel a need to fill a hole in his ego. What is it that makes a man think that something is missing?

A truth I realized after being married for a year is that my wife is constantly changing. I sometimes think that my wife is a different woman. If a man pays attention to his wife; he will realize that she is constantly changing. I never feel the need to sleep with another woman. My wife changes so much I am never bored. I like receiving attention from other women, but I don't have to have sex with them to be fulfilled. I believe there is a better joy that results from perfecting a bond with one woman.

The man who is satisfied with himself will not be inclined to cheat on his wife. The wise man will understand that his marriage will make him a better person. He must operate with restraint. He can never heal himself while sharing his body with other women.

Another family lie that alters a person's world view is the excuse people use when confronted with the truth. The excuse people use is heard often. When a child says my condition is my parents fault; he or she is telling half the truth. It is a fact that our parents influence a large part of our lives. Most of us only know what our parents teach us. When we become teens, we start to look at the world through our own eyes. This is when we rise or fall.

I know how teenagers begin to lose their direction in life when high school starts. This is when the disillusionment sets in. The view of the world offered by our parents loses its strength. My friends and I started to reject our parent's view of the world. I still remember when I felt lied to about the world. The problem with losing faith is that the human mind is already corrupted by the time we reach high school. Some of our problems are the result of imperfect parents. Most of it is our lack of proper decision making. But I already mentioned earlier; we do not get everything we deserve.

"It is my parent's fault I ended up like this." I see this attitude reflected on television. I used this excuse before. It is half-true. I can blame them for certain decisions they made. I can say that they did not provide what I wanted all the time. But what about my own choices. What about the other boys I grew up with who had no parents? It is too easy to blame parents.

Some children had the same situation as other children and they succeeded. Many orphans took the few opportunities they were offered and made good lives for themselves. We all should stop lying on our parents. What if we stopped blaming others for our failures? What if we just accepted life for what it is? It is not fair and we should take more responsibility for our destinies.

Be honest with yourself. If your life is not what you desire; why are you living that life? You chose that life. What changes can you make to improve your life? Now you know that you cannot change your whole life alone. Ask your family members to help you. If you are married; ask your spouse to help you.

You cannot change every aspect of your character. You need the Lord Jesus Christ to guide you through the personal transformation.

# DISHONESTY

The world of deception only exists because of dishonesty. Dishonesty is the opposite of honesty. Honesty is defined by Merriam Webster as the absence of deception. Deception is defined by Merriam Webster as the act of compelling someone else to believe something that is not real. Dishonesty is the reason people live with fear. Dishonesty is the source of all rebellion.

The lies we live with produce the alternate reality we choose to be our real lives. Men and women do not want to accept their true selves. Our alternate reality is sometimes better than the actual truth. This false world consists of ideas and concepts that allow us to live in peace. It is a plain human peace. That peace only lasts as long as no one confronts you about it. I have experienced this point of discomfort myself.

When I arrive at church, people will see the real me. If my clothes are tacky, people will see it. If my car is dirty, people will see it. If my children are wearing dingy clothes, everyone will see them. If I am fat and sloppy, everyone will notice. How often do we avoid the public eye because of shame?

Dishonesty is an unhealthy practice. Dishonesty leads to fear and anxiety. Anxiety is the cause of substance abuse and mental disorders. Men and women who subscribe to a life of deception will experience negative effects on their mind. Physical ailments will manifest themselves as a result of living the dishonest life. The Bible has a verse that talks about how the guilty man runs away; even if there is no one chasing him.

Dishonesty is not a half-truth. Dishonesty is totally wrong. Dishonesty is totally false. The worst aspect of dishonesty is the way it alters the condition of the soul. When I was living a few lies, I became a different person. I literally became a half-truth. I personified a real me and a fake me; at the same time. The real me used my government name.

The other me used whatever name was convenient for the moment.

When I was living this life, I had a few nicknames. I always wondered why I had friends who hated their given names. This was a result of their guilty conscience. The real me hated the character that I created to feel free. The fake me loved the new character. The street persona had no responsibility. The real me had to pay bills and report to work every day. Dishonesty produced a split personality.

I wish more men and more women would take the time to analyze themselves. How many people are living inside your mind at this present moment? You will know that more than one of you exists if you have nicknames. You will know more than one of you exists if you can never explain your decisions. You will know that more than one of you exists if you are bisexual. A person with more than one persona will always be at odds with his or herself.

At one point in time, I was changing religious affiliations. I was a Christian man. Then I was agnostic. Then I was a 5% per center Muslim. Then I attempted to be a Muslim. Then I started studying I-Ching. This book introduced me to Hinduism. My soul was searching for something.

Men, women, and children must begin living lives that consist of no lying. Stop lying. What would happen if every person told the truth about every incident? The first thing that would happen is; people would stop and think before they committed an act. They would start thinking more and doing less. We would not do the things we do if we had to tell the truth all of the time. Telling the truth would scare us into righteous living.

Telling the truth would also remove the dishonesty our relationships are based on. How many friends do you have for the wrong reasons? How many friends do you keep around because you need something from them but you do not need them? How many men have female friends who love them because of a lie? How many women keep men on post by lying to them: just so she can use them? I have been a party to most of these situations.

I lied to women about whatever she wanted to believe. It was fun. I did not need to lie, but it added to the drama. Some women want to be mesmerized. The storytelling was mostly entertainment. I did not need dishonesty to get what I wanted from women. The storytelling was just a part of the different characters I manifested to live my duplicitous life.

I had women lie to me and use me. I learned how to tell relationship lies from girls. When I was in middle school, a lot of girls decided to live their music video fantasies. This is when the games started for me. This is when I learned the game. We had no pagers and cell phones back then. No Facebook and no internet. It was easy to have more than one girlfriend. It was easy for a girl to have more than one boyfriend.

These games were fun to play. I never took it personal. It was just childish entertainment at this point. I knew when a woman was lying. I just wanted to win the contest of deception. It is a game. That is why we call ourselves players. No one was looking for a husband or wife at this point. What we did not realize was this season of our lives set the foundation for a future of deceit. Dishonesty usually begins in a harmful manner.

Dishonest people are not accepted anywhere. No one wants to be in fellowship with a liar. If you ask anyone if he or she likes to associate with liars; he or she will say no. But those people are usually liars themselves. The difference is the severity of the lie. The difference is the motive behind the lie. I hated liars and thieves, but I was a liar and a thief.

We usually justify the fables that serve our self-righteous purpose. Another lie we accept. It is okay if I lie because I wanted to avoid trouble. It is okay if I steal; as long as I don't get caught. We say things like that. We justify our wicked behavior and condemn others for doing the same thing. Why? We exist in the world of deception.

I am convinced we like the world of deception. It is the only place where humans have total control. It is the only place where we do not have to submit to God. Many of our problems are the result of not submitting to God. The truth, the whole truth, and nothing but the truth is this. It is Jesus Christ or darkness.

We try to make a third world. But it does not work. Trust me I tried. The Bible said it is better to never know him than it is to know him and walk away. Please trust me. You cannot budget God. I tried. He seeks to be a major part of our lives. That is why we enjoy the world of deception. It excludes God.

## STREET LIES

I remember when I was living the street life. I remember when I spent hours on the block. I remember when I was up all night selling crack. I remember driving all over Newport News meeting customers. The street life was fun. The street life was exciting. The street life was an adrenaline rush. The street life was deadly. That is the whole truth. You can get killed in the streets. Many half-truths are taught about the street life. The whole truth is that it is deadly.

The streets are deadly. The streets are occupied by dead men. The streets are full of dead thieves, dead addicts, dead prostitutes, dead pimps, and dead drug dealers. Dead people surrounded by dead people produces more death. Death plus death equals death. How can dead people produce life? The only answer is Jesus. They need to know Jesus.

I was involved in the streets because of the money, freedom, position, and power. It appeared to be a way out of my misery. The truth is that I was miserable because I did not know the Lord. I went from one dead condition to another dead condition.

I actually thought I was bringing life to the block. Life is Jesus. But it was Jesus we really did not want. That made me a hypocrite. Of course I did not realize this at the time. But we cannot be made alive and free without Him. I was the hypocrite. I wanted to be alive in a dead game. I wanted to be alive in the dead streets. I was the hypocrite.

This spiritual war caused me to never fit in. I was too smart to obey school teachers. I was too skeptical to submit to church folk. I was too rebellious to hang out with Christian kids. And I was too spiritual to fit in with the street thugs.

I was not aware that the Creator will not let his son fit into a place that he does not belong. I did not know that maybe, just maybe, God himself was preventing me from fitting in. The idea of "getting in where you fit in" is a good concept to acknowledge. But it is a half-truth because all of us do not fit in with this world. The other flaw in this concept is that we constantly change.

A changing person should never attempt to fit into a place. The fitting will prevent change and growth. Pain and frustration will grow as a result of fitting in. a man should only attempt to fit into an institution that is an organism and not an organization. Organisms are alive and constantly changing. Organizations are not alive and do not consistently grow. An organism that grows is the living church of God. An organism is a charity that operates with compassion and love. An organization is a gang with strict leadership. They operate through fear and intimidation.

A man can grow in a church because it nurtures his gifts and gives him freedom to make choices. A gang will manipulate its members and force them to commit criminal acts. If a man disagrees with his church, he can pray be at peace. If a man disagrees with his gang, he may be hit or excommunicated. An organism will allow a person to grow on his own and with the body. An organization will kill a person who does not want to be a part of the body. It will view the former member as an opponent. Opponents must be eradicated.

I was accepted by everyone but not connected to anyone. I never understood this phenomena as a child. I never understood the loneliness I experienced as an adult. There were times I wanted to belong to something. I wanted to fit in somewhere. I was tired of seeing everyone else enjoy their teams and cliques. I was growing frustrated with seeing everyone else live in harmony. I always thought I was missing something. I felt like I was living my life as a window shopper. I could not understand why I was so close to so many people but not attached. I discovered the answer later.

"Get in where you fit in." Be careful where you fit in. What if fitting in cost you your soul? What if fitting in stopped you from growing? The only thing worse than an untimely death is living and not growing. A man who is firmly fit in a position will not be able to grow because his personal growth will remove him from his current position. Be careful.

What drives a man to fit into a gang or clique? What would cause a man to desire a position that may stop his rise to his proper destiny? The simple answers are all involved in what he thinks he is missing. Gang recruiters take advantage of a person's feelings of inadequacy. If a young man thinks he is missing authority or power, he will seek to fulfill it in gang. A positive method of fulfillment is a sports team or vocation.

Another half-truth in the street life is the notion of, "this is my block." Who started that idea? Why do people think that they own something? I understand the mentality that promotes this type of thinking. We think just because we live in this neighborhood and grew up on this street, that it belongs to us. But the truth is that most of the street thugs live in a neighborhood that is paid for by the fathers and mothers who work every day. The working adults are paying the bills. How is it that the kids on the corner claim ownership? If it is your hood, why do you run from the police? Why do your parents pay rent?

"This is my block." This statement is a half-truth. I deceived myself in the past believing I had some influence in my neighborhood. I claimed ownership of a territory before. I loved my neighborhood. I had many friends in my neighborhood. We fought cliques from other neighborhoods that came to start trouble. I was taught to fight for my neighborhood. It was an easy way to earn respect. It was not easy to fight but the respect was immediately earned afterwards. But it was not our neighborhood. I learned this the hard way. We all learned this the hard way.

In 1993, the association that operated Courthouse Green removed the basketball court from the park in the back of the neighborhood. The entire basketball court was removed. The first step was the removal of the basketball goals. The black top remained. We waited for the goals to be put back on the backboards. It never happened. A few months after the goals were removed, the whole blacktop was dug out of the ground. I will never forget that event. Our whole neighborhood changed. This event taught me the true definition of power. The children who ran the streets did not have any power.

This event started with a newsletter being delivered to every home. The newsletter talked about the violence and drug crimes being committed in the neighborhood. The residents who did not participate in the hip-hop lifestyle or participate in the street culture complained that the park was the central location for the negative behaviors. The basketball court hosted drug dealers. Cars used to park in the cul-de-sac and blast loud music. A lot of local drug dealers visited the basketball court. Some of us played football on the field next to the basketball court. This was the spot. I did not sell drugs in 1993. I just wanted to. I dreamed of having money.

The newsletter informed the residents that many of the families in the area wanted to reduce crime and vacate the drug dealers. The idea was to stop unwanted guests from entering the community. The association had a vote to decide if removing the basketball court would curb violence and drug dealing. A few weeks later, the basketball goals were gone. This taught me and my friends that the street thugs had no power. We felt violated. Some of us still played football in the field but the park was never the same after the basketball court was gone.

Crime was reduced after this event. Less traffic from other neighborhoods created a decrease in incidents. Ironically, this event increased mischief among the native residents. Outsiders did not enter as much. There was no place to play basketball. But the people who lived there started getting into criminal activity.

Ask yourself; do you really own your neighborhood? Do you truly run the streets? I know a lot of notorious criminals who impress the kids younger than them because of an old reputation; but very few of them have absolute power.

I do not believe the thugs who say, this is my block. Who is paying the rent? Who owns the land? The areas that are controlled by gangs have residents who still pay rent. If these families stop paying the rent, they will be evicted. Who really owns the street? Images control the minds of the weak. Do not let those images deceive you. The drug dealers in my neighborhood could not stop the association from removing the basketball court.

How many times have you heard someone say that no one comes from our hood and succeeds in the white man's world? I remember hearing that statement hundreds of times. I saw a lot of movies that depressed me when I was growing up. These movies were very negative. I allowed the negative message to put fear in my heart. I started to think that I would never achieve my high aspirations. I began to think that I was not supposed to be prosperous. I let outside influences stifle my hope.

If you read what I just wrote, you will see that I stated, "I let", "I allowed." I am responsible for my decisions. We are not always responsible for our environments.

I lived in Denbigh. This section of Newport News is populated by shipyard employees, military soldiers, and military families. Denbigh was not the worst section of the city. But we did have our rough neighborhoods.

I did not want to enlist in the military. But the military appeared to be the only option for me. I knew I did not want to go to the Army. I knew I did not want a dead end job. But I was also afraid to go to college. College was a very high goal for me and my friends. For some reason college was a supreme step to make. College was the equivalent of a football player winning the Super Bowl. I cannot explain why my mind viewed college as something impossible. I now realize that I could have easily attended college.

My fear of college began with a half-truth. My anxiety about college is also a symptom of not believing that a regular black man from a crime filled neighborhood could achieve a high dream. I learned to lose from several sources. I wish I never accepted the idea that I could not win. I wish I never became comfortable being a loser. The half-truth was, "If you go to college and you not an athlete, you will become a sell-out." I remember being told that college would make me white. The fear of losing friends and fitting into the white man's world produced doubt and self-destructive behavior. What was I really afraid of? Where did this fear come from?

The fear of being great is implanted in many men and women at an early age. The ideas that we had early in our lives to be awesome were greeted with opposition. The fear of being great was implanted into me and some of my friends by older black people who were failures in their own lives. I wonder if these people were oppressing us on purpose. I wonder if they knew that they were damaging our minds. I can remember telling myself I don't deserve to win. It is painful to admit this now.

How does a child learn to be good if he or she is told that it is impossible? How can a child become great if his or hers true inspiration is extinguished early in life? I never tell my sons that they cannot win. I never tell them what they cannot do. I tell them how to prepare for their futures. I help them train for their sports. I taught my first son to read and perform mathematical equations. I remind them that any dream is possible. Ironically, I am probably lying to my sons when I tell them that they can do anything and accomplish any goal.

Some ideas are too big. But almost everything else is possible. An example is telling my sons that they can become Black presidents. Every Black boy in America cannot be a Black president. But thousands of fathers tell their sons that it is possible. But the truth is that all of our black boys will never be politicians. Regardless, I never tell my children what they cannot do. I keep them dreaming.

I had most of my dreams extinguished at an early age. It took me years to become confident again. It took me years to learn how to walk by faith again. The idea that only the gifted, rich, and lucky kids will be successful in life is half true. I had my hope and my faith damaged because I thought I was not supposed to win. I attempted to balance my religion with the things I learned in the streets. Many times it was the religious people who did not want me to win. I still cannot explain that hatred.

The reason that gifted, rich, and lucky children win is because they are associated with other people who win. When winners get together, they produce more wins. Winners will fellowship with other winners because it compels them to keep winning. The gifted ones win because their gifts create opportunities. The rich children get ahead in life because the money affords them the best teachers and coaches. The lucky ones win because of chance and unplanned encounters. I have met some lucky people. The most important element that allows the gifted, rich, and lucky to prosper is good decision making. A son or daughter of a wealthy couple can choose to commit crime or abuse drugs. That is the truth.

Many gifted, rich, and lucky men are in prison right now. People do not rob, steal, and kill because they are poor. That is a lie. People rob, steal, and kill because of the flaws in their character. Circumstances may produce criminal thoughts; but the heart of a person must be wicked to commit the immoral acts.

Life is about making proper decisions. The people who make the proper decisions at the appropriate times will be productive and effective in this world. It does not matter which religion or faith you subscribe to; the best decision makers prosper in the end. We all will face challenges in this life. We will all make mistakes in this life. The ones who work hard and educate themselves will become winners. These successful people will be able to prepare their children for success. This is not a half-truth.

I had plenty of reasons for accepting a life less than I deserved. The negativity was always present. The half-truth is that maybe I wanted to struggle. Maybe I wanted to start from the bottom and elevate to the top. Maybe I liked the low life because it allowed me to avoid responsibility. The media and the church preachers always glorify the negativity. The only time I heard something positive was when I was among white people. But I was taught not to trust them. (I can write a whole book about how I was taught not to trust white people. But I can name several white men who did everything they could to help me do something great with my life.)

The same people who complain about the negative effect of crime and drugs also do a great job promoting it. The first time I saw crack and weed was at my elementary school. My friends and I went home and wondered where we could find those drugs. I understand that they intended to educate children about the damage that can be caused by drug abuse but sometimes they only provoked experimentation.

Too many negative messages are delivered in churches. I heard a lot more fearful messages in church than educational messages. I remember leaving church with more questions and confusion than answers and inspiration. I remember leaving church and feeling anxious and scared. I never left powerful. I worried about things that never happened. I wonder how many other children left church filled with doubt, fear, worry, and depressed. I was afraid of the streets until those thugs became my friends.

It amazes me how the ones we seek for comfort are the same ones who promote more negativity. We go to church and seek answers from elders and counselors but sometimes they only remind us of the problems. When I started to spend time with the street thugs, they provided ideas and answers. The answers were sometimes wrong but a lost man will listen to another lost man because he identifies with him.

The truth is that this life is unfair. This life will depress a man. This life will sometimes break a man. This life will expose every good thing in a man. This life will expose every negative thing within a man. These are truths. But we still have decisions to make.

This is something that I used to say all the time, "I can't leave my people behind." For some reason, I did not want to prosper if my friends did not prosper. I hear some of the inmates in my facility repeat this concept. They do not want to do better if their gang members are suffering. I have taken losses to remain among my friends. The streets is a state of bondage. One of my greatest regrets is related to the idea that the streets were my home. Even though I did not belong there.

One of my biggest regrets is missing out on the opportunity to own my own business. I had an opportunity to manage my own restaurant. In 1997, I worked at a McDonalds in Staunton, Va. The manager of the restaurant and the area manager noticed my work ethic and my independence. One day I asked the area manager why he was going out of town every couple weeks. He informed me that he was flying to the McDonalds corporate office for training purposes. I asked him why he had to leave Virginia to fly to Chicago for training. He told me that the training allowed him to earn more money and get the necessary certifications to own his own restaurant.

The longer I worked at McDonalds; the more I did not like it. I enjoyed the challenge of running the grill area alone. I liked being able to serve hundreds of people by myself, but I felt that McDonalds was a clowns job. I was 19 years old at the time. I was full of pride, arrogance, and that hip-hop attitude. I allowed the images of the media and the negativity of my friends at that time make me think I was in the wrong line of work. I was not considering my future. I did not plan to live past the age of 21. I was told that I would not live past the age of 21.

The manager and the area manager of the restaurant both told me that I can be promoted to an assistant manager position. They both told me that I can be trained to become a supervisor. I thought about that idea and procrastinated with a decision. I asked a lot of questions about the responsibilities of a manager. The area manager told me that once I became a restaurant manager, I would receive training in all the safety regulations and the federal laws regarding payroll, taxes, and food safety. He was flying to the Chicago area to get higher training because he was planning on relocating to another state to be responsible for a fleet of restaurants. I was 19 years old and being offered an opportunity to be groomed as a corporate boss. What would you have done?

I remember this season of my life like it was yesterday. I remember how I felt at the age of 19. I told the manager I did not want to be a manager. I just wanted to move back to Newport News. I was in Staunton serving a parole sentence in a halfway house. I was leaving Staunton in less than six months. I could have stayed there and become a manager. It is now 2014. I could have been a corporate executive by now. I only had to allow my mind to be reformed.

I did not accept this opportunity. I did not allow that white man to lead me on a path to prosperity. I did not allow that white man to teach me the corporate world. I was not ready to leave my ghetto, stupid mentality behind and become a wise man in the so-called white man's world. This was a mistake. I chose to be relocated back to Newport News.

I did share this idea with a couple people at the time. Those people did not encourage me to go that route. It is a shame that young black men are surrounded by older black people who did not chase their dreams. I wish I could have encountered someone who told me to do it.

A couple of negative ideas prevented me from accepting this social promotion. The lies we live with influence our thinking without us asking it to happen. These subconscious ideas emerge effortlessly. These ideas are called prejudice and bias. These ideas are usually fortified by pride.

One of the ideas focused on debt. I did not want to feel like I owed the manager anything. I wanted to work my up. I did not want to owe him anything. I did not want him to think he owned me. In reality, he never viewed the situation in that manner. He just identified a faithful worker who can function without constant supervision. My fear and pride compelled me to remain at a distance from the man who attempted to make me wealthy and powerful.

The other idea that hindered my elevation was the street lie about selling out. I felt like a traitor accepting a job in Stanton, Va. If this opportunity was offered in Newport News or Hampton, I probably would have accepted it. But this chance was delivered in Staunton. I did not want to be separated from my friends. This is why I never use the term "down with my team" any more. I will never be "DOWN" again. Staying down with the team will literally hold a man down.

The most damaging lie that I mentioned in the past is the one that altered my whole worldview. I had this deep down conviction that I would never live past the age of 21. This conviction caused me so much harm; I ruined many phases of my life. The idea that I would live past 21 destroyed hundreds of my hopes and dreams. The idea that I would not live past the age of 21 damaged hundreds of my friendships. The idea that I would not live past the age of 21 caused me to give up on people, faith, religion, family, my health, and imagination. I will talk more about that later. In this instance, I missed a golden opportunity to enhance my life. I am still suffering from this misfortune.

Many times we only accept gifts and promotions if they come from a person who receives our approval. If the manager was another young black man who listened to Wu-tang music; I probably would have followed him. The reality is that most executives do not subscribe to the street, hip-hop lifestyle. That is why we have to be willing to change ourselves in order to grow up. No man can enter into the king role with a slave's mentality.

Years past by before I realized how this opportunity and other choices I made were related to one lie I accepted. We all must analyze our perception of the world. One lie can ruin your whole existence. One lie can make a man or woman believe that he or she is doing the right thing but he or she is in fact damaging his or herself. Just one lie.

## THE AGE OF 21

I was raised in church. I was similar to other children. I was forced to go to church. I never wanted to be there. I received positive messages on some occasions. I heard a lot about God and Jesus and Heaven and Hell. I believed what I was supposed to believe. Inside my soul I knew a God was real. I just never allowed that idea to dominate my real life. God was a personal fantasy that remained detached from my real life. Every time I tried to incorporate God into my life, I was hurt or disappointed.

I also heard confusing and negative messages in church. I would hear messages about how good God was but then I would be told that he is angry and mad. These types of contradictions always left me with a sense of insecurity. Children should never be filled with insecurity in a church. I remember when a preacher once told the congregation that Black boys would not reach the age of 21. I heard this from a Black preacher. I still remember the event. I still remember how I felt that night. I hated it. I internalized it.

My question is, "why would he say something like that?" Does God know I will not reach the age of 21? What made me susceptible to believing that I would not live that long?

I mentioned this state of mind in my first book. I am rehashing this idea because I am not the only man or woman who feels this way. I am not the only Black boy who heard that statement. I wonder how many other men or women are willing to admit that their life expectancy was 21 years of age. The most essential aspect of this negative prophecy is that I never consciously realized how real it was to me. The thought would come up in my mind. Every now and then I would say it. But I never recognized the stronghold it had on my life.

I was tormented by the idea that I would not live long. In a way I was freed by this prophecy too. Maybe people do not reveal their fears because they actually free them from responsibility. Maybe the lies we accept are designed to expose our flaws. Maybe I did not want to live past 21. I don't know. I really don't know.

I can admit that I was freed by the idea that God would take me away at 21. It would give me an excuse not to go to college. It gave me the excuse not to buy a house or begin a long-term rewarding career. It also allowed me to avoid long-term relationships with women. I did not look for a wife. I never really thought about building with a woman. I searched for entertainment and immediate gratification with women. I had several chances to attend college before my 21st birthday. I walked away from them. I remember saying that it was a waste of time. This lie was a tool I used to avoid responsibility.

I often wonder why a preacher would tell a congregation that the Black boys had a very small chance to live past the age of 21. What would this type of sensationalism accomplish? I hope the preachers who share that type of message realize the damage it causes. When I preach to teenagers who do not know the Jesus; I don't give them doom and gloom topics. Their lives are already doom and gloom. I give them messages with hope and clarity. I attempt to teach them that their condition can change now. I share the concept that Jesus will give them purpose. Now!

Many other ideas and subconscious thoughts are manipulated when I consider how I believed this lie. Maybe I wanted to believe the lie. It is also true that the religion I was immersed in propagated the prophecy. I was constantly warned that I may not see tomorrow. The same religious leaders who tell children not to live for the moment; are the same religious leaders who say that "no one is promised tomorrow." Conflicting message. I lived a high risk life for years. I could not dream of being an old, family man.

This entire disposition of mine was a form of cognitive dissonance too. I claimed that I may not live long.

I had the implanted fear. But I also wanted to be good. I wanted everyone to like me. I wanted to be remembered for treating people right. If I really did not plan to live long, why would I care about everyone else's feelings? Why didn't I join the Marines and jump out of airplanes?

I did get involved in some illegal activity. I did get involved in a lot of violence. But I never lost control of my sanity. I wish I could explain my whole disposition at the time. Maybe if I had a medical diagnosis I would have been labeled bipolar. I was either elated or depressed. The events and actions that should have made me happy; made me sad. The events and actions that should have made me sad; made me happy. This sounds weird doesn't it?

The events that make the mentally healthy person happy did not make me happy. Peace, prosperity, and love contradicted what I thought life was supposed to be. I was afraid to be totally happy and content. That would have made me want to live a long joyful life. I had to ruin anything that would make me want to live long. I had to die young and go see Jesus. Maybe then I would be happy.

The events that make the mentally healthy person sad did not make me sad. The negative events made me content and happy. It just proved that the negative prophecy was true. After all, I heard it in church. I heard the negative prophecy in church more than one time. I lived with no responsibility and a lack of restraint. Like I said before, I still didn't lose my mind.

God Himself restrained me in a lot of situations. I can reminisce and see how God prevented me from doing a lot of extremely stupid things. I also remember how God would remove people from my life at critical times. Wild women and stupid men were taken from my life at vulnerable moments. I had some opportunities to make thousands of dollars overnight. But these people would just disappear. In the early 90's, we had no cellphones and Facebook. It was easy to lose contact with someone.

Sometimes I think that our new technologies are from the enemy of our souls. It is almost impossible to get away from people now. I lost contacts in the 90's that I would not lose if I was a teenager today. But that is something I will write about in another book.

I lived with a lot of fear. I lived with a lot of anger. I lived with a lot of bitterness. I had some medical problems that hindered my life. Bad knees and asthma made it hard for me to play sports. I still tried. Religion made me not trust people. I still tried. School was a waste of time. All we did in school was fight each other and tell lies. The boys and the girls did the same thing. Fight and tell lies. The best actor or the best fighter was the one with the most props. Sometimes the best athlete would be well-respected. I was none of them. I was somewhere in the middle.

The problem with a Heaven based religion is it prevents a weak person from establishing anything of substance while on Earth. It will cause that person to despise this life and just wait to die. That person becomes a doormat to everyone else. If it is a man; he loses his manhood and dignity. If it is a woman; she loses her self-respect and becomes insecure. Both of them become prey for: cults, gangs, secret clubs, and any charismatic person who can make him or her feel good about his or herself. I learned that most of the cults, gangs, and secret fraternities are full of former Christians and Muslims who were indoctrinated early in life.

I do agree that there is an afterlife with God. I do believe in a Heaven or Hell scenario after death. But I also believe in a purpose here on Earth. We experience the presence of God here on Earth. We can do something good while we are here. Instead of telling a child he will die at an early age because he is Black; tell him how he can pray and change that situation. What if those preachers told me that God would fill me with the Holy Spirit and show me how to stop Black boys from dying at an early age? That is a life of purpose. Not a life of insignificance and insecurity. I would have had a reason to live.

Live with a purpose. Do not wait to die. There is a difference.

What lie are you living with? Did you receive a disturbing message at a church? Find some good teachers and elders. Ask for discipleship and counseling. Grow properly and avoid a life of self-destruction. I would encourage all men (and young women) to engage in discipleship. If your church does not offer discipleship, get out. We cannot grow without help. If you don't have a church; find a church with a teacher who preaches.

I developed a pattern of defeating myself. That pattern was fortified by public images of the good guy gone wrong. My pattern of self-destruction was reinforced by images on television. Ricky in the movie *Boys n the Hood* reinforced the idea that good boys die young. Tre reinforced the idea that the weak and scared get lucky. Who wanted to be weak and scared?

The hip-hop music in the 90's reinforced thousands of negative ideas. I cannot list all of the evil we ingested from the music. I will just write about one major element. This element is the death lyrics. All hip-hop music is not detrimental to the health of the listener. But the death lyrics are evil. The dark, death message must be removed. I listened to a lot of the dark, death sound.

I could not laugh and dance to Hammer and Puff Daddy songs. I was too depressed. The negative death sound was my theme music. I needed it to maintain my cognitive dissonance. I had to remain unhappy. Music is more than a sound. Music contains a spirit. Music alters the attitude. Music has the power of attraction. If we both like the same song, we must be alike.

I still remember going to a party at a nightclub in 1997. I was 19 years old. The DJ was playing music by different artists. I can still remember this moment. Like it happened last night. The DJ played the song *Triumph*, by the Wutang Clan. Almost everyone in the club that night stood up to dance. The very next song was *Been Around the World*, by Puff Daddy and Mase. Everyone walked off the dance floor. I still remember this moment. It had to be a lesson for me from Heaven. Why did everyone refuse to dance to that song?

The reason we all walked off the dance floor is because we were not living the life Puff Daddy and Mase was living. The year was 1997. The city was Newport News. It is easy to go buckwild for the Wutang Clan music because we all were in the struggle. We knew each other from the surrounding neighborhoods. I was just released from prison and parole that year. Relating to the Wutang sound was easy. But none of us were rich pimps and players like Puff Daddy and Mase. We could not relate to that image.

The other factor is weakness. Whoever wanted to dance to that music would have become a target. Most of us were not wealthy. We were living check-to-check. Some of us did not have jobs. The people who chose to front like they were rich; would have been robbed or assaulted. That was the reality at this point in time. I saw it for myself. This club did not have a high security presence. The party scene in 1997 was different than it is now. The ones who thought they were better than everyone else would get robbed and assaulted every weekend. The clubs that protected the wannabee "players" were not in my neighborhood.

This incident highlighted another issue in our culture. Why are we jealous of the people who are prosperous? Why is it wrong for them to succeed? We sing about success. We sing about being rich. We talk about spoiling women and increasing our wealth. But when someone actually does it; he or she is treated like an enemy by his or hers own people.

Jealousy and envy are dangerous. I will write about those two issues in another book. I felt envy and jealousy before. It cost me some healthy relationships. I lost good friends because of my insecurity. Regret. I thought it was unfair for others to do well and I couldn't. Living with a lie. I did have permission to succeed. Somehow, I trained myself to fail.

God loved me so much; He moved me to Georgia. God knew I needed to change my environment because I refused to change in Newport News. This new geographical area allowed me to think and be free. I was not bound by my reputation in Georgia. I had a chance to start over. Without peer pressure; I should have been able to think clear. I wish it was that easy to change my mentality. I wish a change of address could correct the heart. It didn't.

I moved to the Atlanta area and found hundreds of other angry Black men. I continued with my negative thinking. I continued getting high and drunk. The closer I arrived to my 21$^{st}$ birthday; the more erratic my behavior became. I was afraid of my birthday. I did not know why. I mentioned this incident in my first book. I had this curse on me that I failed to identify.

I had a nervous breakdown on August 25, 1999. This is the date of my 21$^{st}$ birthday. When I realized that I would not die; I did not know what to do. I just cried. All of the negative images, ideas, and fears flashed through my mind. All I could hear was a voice saying, "I told you. I told you I would protect you." I am obviously paraphrasing. It is impossible to quote God verbatim. But that is how I felt. That is the relief and shame I experienced at the moment. I did not think I would ever see that day.

The week before it came, I was extremely nervous. I was constantly waiting for something bad to happen. Nothing happened. This experience was a new beginning in my life. This experience was the beginning of the cleansing of my mind. I had to relearn what to think, believe, and know. I had to relearn how to live by faith.

Faith became essential when I reached the age of 21. I believe God wanted me to know he carried me through all of my depression and attempted self-destruction. Faith became essential because I did not have a plan. I had no idea what to do with my life. I never saw this far ahead. Now what?

## THE PLAYER

Some of the deception we live with appears harmless. Some of the deception is associated with entertainment and imagination. These subtle deviances in reality may appear to be harmless but they cause a lifetime of pain. One innocent lie is the concept of "the Player." It is a lie that a man must be a "Player" to be measured as certified. It is a lie that a man must sleep with a hundred women to be considered legit. It is a lie that a virgin is weird or suspect.

I am not saying that this game is not real. I am saying that the lie involves a role playing that produces deceit. The man and the woman in the game become liars and deceivers. The game is real. Casual sex is real. Recreational dating is real. The evidence is seen by the large amount of single parent homes. The evidence is seen in the lack of commitment. Most of the R&B music is about casual sex and who is using who. I remember some of the old R&B music spoke of marriage and securing bonds. The player/pimp game is real.

I do not have any personal knowledge of pimps and prostitutes. I did encounter elements of that life while living in Atlanta. The prostitution game involves players and pimps. The prostitution game involves women being the players and the pimps. I encountered one prostitute who set me up to be robbed. I also witnessed how invisible the pimps were. I learned a lot about the game.

There is a lot of damage being done to the minds and bodies of those involved. The pimps were cold and calculating. The pimps could not show any feelings. It amazed me to see how much fear the women had towards their pimp. I could never be a pimp. There is a mental slavery involved. The prostitutes were property and not wholly human.

The women suffer damage in this game. Their damage is inside their heart and souls. The game also harms the physical health of the women participating. I met women who were addicted to cocaine. I met women who dishonored themselves just to get attention. They were always operating in a seductive manner. It appeared that these women only viewed themselves as sex objects. The game damages minds. The game of the "player" and "pimp" alters the image of the man and the woman.

The men and women involved in this sex trade may be damaged for life. I know of women who have sexually transmitted diseases that will never be cured. Their lives are forever altered. Millions of men have contracted sexually transmitted diseases in the streets and passed it onto their wives at home.

The lie we live with ruins the lives of those who participate in the sex game. I ruined a lot of good relationships by sleeping with women who were good friends. I ruined a lot of good women by manipulating them. I would start relationships with women just for physical reasons. I was never truly interested in her. I just wanted to use and abuse her. Ironically, women would do the same thing to me. My friends and I were used and manipulated by women for money and security. This happened to me in Virginia and Georgia. Women know that men only want to use their bodies. They were players too.

This system of manipulation produces a culture of deviance and immorality. I wonder if this mental damage is the reason the women take on male attitudes and the men take on female attitudes. Roles are confused and the purpose of the body is changed. The immoral behavior alone will set a person off track. Immoral behavior impairs judgment. Poor judgment leads to self-destruction.

The man is called a player or a pimp if he has his way with multiple women. The woman is called a boss if she has her way with men. I have heard women call themselves players too. Other profane words are substituted for men and women who play the game. I will refrain from the profanity.

We just need to know how much heartbreak is associated with casual sex. No one cares who they hurt. The ones who participate in this sport are usually hurt people. And hurt people hurt people.

Disease is a common issue in the streets. Immoral sexual behavior leads to high levels of infection. AIDS, herpes, and other diseases are spreading at a high rate among teenagers and adults. How many former playboys died from AIDS? How many women who slept with many men for pleasure die from AIDS? Millions more are infected with herpes. Herpes is a disease that will never go away.

The title of' the player" is ascribed to the man who can successfully get his needs met by any woman he chooses. The man who is labeled a "player" can get money, sex, or another form of special treatment from the woman of his choosing. The player is adept at playing the necessary role to achieve his desired end. That end may be physical, material, or emotional. Sometimes a man may just want attention. I had a friend who would walk around school attracting adoration from different girls. He just loved the attention.

The concept of the player is not new. This type of man can be found in any history book that chronicles the social lives of adults. The Bible has examples of men who sought the attention of women in deceptive manners. King David used manipulations to gain access to Bathsheba. The Bible also chronicles the disastrous effect of this illegitimate relationship. The world of deception harms people.

Regardless of how much fun our games may be; people get hurt. A woman cannot share her body with a man that is not her committed husband without being harmed. A man cannot share his body with a woman who is not his wife without being harmed. Our original design was not for casual sex.

I can write about many different reasons the life of a player is destructive. The lie that a man must be able to conquer the opposite sex must be derailed. The definition of a man must come from the one who originally designed the man. The Creator never intended for men to use the bodies of women like toys. The idea is not new. I was indoctrinated into it. My son is being exposed to this idea now. If this idea continues to spread; many more lives will be broken.

The opposite perspective to this is how women are players. How often do women allow men to believe that the man is in control? How often do women allow the man to think that he is influencing her decisions? Women are very deceptive.

Women know exactly what is going on. It is very easy for a woman to sit idly by and watch the man spend money and exalt his own ego. She is doing this because it makes the man feel good. She is doing this to allow him to make more and more reckless decisions. The woman knows that the man cannot function at his prideful level for long. She is already planning her exit strategy. The woman behaves as if the man has the advantage. Her goal is to avoid responsibility. When the money and the power is gone; it will appear as if the man made all the bad decisions. She will leave with no guilt. The life of the Player is lonely. That life is hazardous.

The truth is that every member involved in this fantasy land of sex and partying is guilty. Not only the man and the woman; but the night club owners are guilty. The strip club owners are guilty. The dancers in the clubs are guilty. Many participants are necessary to prolong the life of the casual sex game. This life is a sport. The sport needs a playing field. The sport needs enablers. Everyone is guilty.

The children born from this life are the eventual victims. The children born from this life will endure a lifetime of insecurity. The children will suffer from a distorted view of family and commitment. I meet young men who do not have a positive perception of their existence. This is another incident involving the first lie. A boy who is born without a father will believe that he is not loved. He will accept the lie that, "I am not special." "I am in the way."

The young daughter who is born without a solid family will also suffer. Her mother was misused by a man who only wanted casual sex. The mother misused her own body and allowed the event to take place. Now this woman is on her own with a child. Her purpose in life is derailed. Her goals are altered because of sport sex. This new daughter is now being brought into a situation that is not stable. Her view of the world will be distorted. Her behavior in the presence of men will be tentative or manipulative. She may exhibit both behaviors.

I remember encountering women who are either extra shy or extra aggressive. Both behaviors are an extreme. The woman who appears extra shy is approached by men who are aggressive. The aggressive woman approaches men who can be victimized. Girls and women are players too. The design God intended involved service. That design was completely reversed. The model of dating is now advantage. The one who has the advantage in the relationship is boss. Love was meant to be symbolized by sacrifice; it is now personified by obligation.

The term "Boss" is used by many people when qualifying the terms of the relationship. The one with the advantage is the winner. Service became domination. Once upon a time; the one with the advantage in the relationship was the one who gave the most of his or herself. The goal in the current culture is to get as much as you can before your feelings are hurt by the other party. This mentality has led to the high level of divorce. This mentality has led to the high level of domestic violence. Somehow the culture transformed from giving and we became takers.

This truth is why I believe that the men and the women in this game are not the victims. The men know what they are attempting to get. The women know what the men truly want. So how can either one of them be the victim?

Two willing participants allow themselves to be hurt. I hear the sad R&B songs. I see the complex confusion caused by sitcoms that lead silly women astray. But who are the real victims?

When a woman sleeps with a married man, how can anyone feel pity for her? When a man sleeps with a stripper who already has two baby daddies; why does he think she will honor him? I ask these questions because I engaged in many situations that I knew were bad for my health. I did it anyway because I wanted to see if fire truly burned. I did it to myself.

A good rule to live by is this, "what a man or woman is when you first meet him or her; is who they truly are." First impressions are usually correct. I met some crazy women under wild circumstances. I knew what I was engaging in. I wanted to experiment and see I could change them. I knew I could not change them but I figured it would be an adventure. We only live once. When the pain arrived, I could not complain or cry. I knew she was crazy.

I dated a compulsive liar once. I knew she was a liar from the beginning. I just wanted the adventure and the drama. I wanted to see how the end result would appear. Once again, the first lie seemed to surface in my life. When I was a child and saw how the actors in the movies received second chances. I remembered how the actors in the movie were able to come back to life with no consequence. I wanted to see if this lying woman would ever tell the truth. I did not realize that the time I was wasting on her would never be returned.

I did not realize how that experience would impact every relationship I entered into with future women. Ladies and gentlemen, brothers and sisters; we must learn to heed the warnings in the Bible. Every person we expose ourselves to will alter our point of reference. Every person we become intimate with will alter our point of comfort. Every person we share our hearts with will alter our point of discomfort. Every relationship will distort our point of revelation. This is the truth.

I had trouble trusting women for years because of this woman. I didn't even know it at the time. My world view shifted with my permission because I had to have this woman. The lie is that I thought I can change her. The lie is that I thought I could handle it without my heart being affected. Those are both lies. Everyone gets hurt in the end. I have never met an unhappy virgin.

When did you change your world view? How many of your own rules did you break because you wanted something that you knew was bad for you? How many of your values did you release because you wanted to embark on an adventure? One question, were you the same person when the adventure was over? No.

The true victims of sport sex are the children. The children who are born from this lifestyle are not the only victims. Fatherless children will experience enormous pressure in this world. Motherless children will experience enormous pressure in this world. The True and Living God knew what it would take to maintain order on this Earth. One man, one woman, One God. The unsupervised children creating havoc in the streets are the result of failed relationships. There is no such thing as a victimless sin.

I volunteer at a juvenile prison. The facility is stocked with children who lacked proper supervision. These children caused havoc in the streets; which affected the lives of the people who lived in their community. That havoc altered the lives of their neighbors. Those neighbors had stress, fear, and anxiety that was caused by the immoral behavior of the parents of those wild children. This is a vicious cycle. The children who are born out of wedlock affect the other children in the community who may have whole families. The irresponsible adults who produce unsupervised children must realize that their actions affect every family that lives near them.

There is no victimless crime. There is no victimless sin. The life of the player does have consequences. I hear men complain about child support. I hear women complain about feeling abandoned. That situation could have been avoided. Now the child suffers. When a child suffers, the whole community suffers. This entire scenario was spawned by one lie. "I am a Player."

The children who witness others engage in this lifestyle are also the victims. The children who see the game on television will adopt some of the behaviors. The children who see the lies and deceit involved in the game will adopt those traits. It happened to me. It also happened to my friends. We learned to lie and cheat by watching adults. A teenager never looks 10 years down the road to see the possible consequences.

Some of my friends and I had parents who were married. We witnessed what a whole family is supposed to look like. We could have followed that model. The challenge is finding a good model to pattern your future after. Good family models are hard to find. Most of us see the flaws in our families. We never see the answers.

I remember meeting good girls. It was hard to trust them because I expected the good act to end. Most of us expected to be played and manipulated by the women we met. This expectation made us learn how to deceive them first. We positioned ourselves in a manner to avoid receiving a broken heart. Everything was a game. Unfortunately, even when I met a good woman; the opportunity to start something real vanished because of the game.

I can write an entire book about the image of a relationship. That is another study all by itself. Boys and girls date each other because of the appearance in the cafeteria. Neither one of them truly loves each other. Adults do the same thing on a different level. Women look for men who can provide a particular service or a specific need. Men want a woman who will not expect him to change. It is still a game to them.

The point that is important to know is how a distorted view of the purpose of a relationship leads to moral and spiritual decay. This moral and spiritual decay leads to the decay of the traditional family. These elements are then passed on to other people. When a man with a wrong view teaches a younger man how to treat a woman: what happens? The cycle continues.

## HOLLYWOOD LIES

The television is the easiest entity to blame for our social problems. I admit, anyone can blame the television for his or hers dysfunctional life. I have used the media as an excuse for my bad decisions. I have no problem admitting that there were moments I was not mature enough to accept responsibility for negative choices I made. I had to point the finger at something. This is similar to the religious people who blame the Devil for their situations. At what point do we all say, "I made a mistake." Life is always pleasant after admitting fault. When a person admits his or hers own failures, there are no accusers pointing fingers at him or her. I have learned to admit my errors. Sometimes you should just plead guilty.

That is my disclaimer. Now I want to expose some of the brainwashing that is conducted by Hollywood. Hollywood does have the tools to brainwash people. Hollywood does have the ability to control the minds of the masses. Anyone who says that the television does not impact their decisions is a liar. That man or woman is in denial. The truth is that the ideas peddled through the media are influential. The lie is that they have no mind control power. The other truth is that the men and women who watch television still have the authority to control their actions.

Everyone knows that the media is an influence in our lives. Men and women watch television because we want to be told what is real and fake. Men and women watch television because we want distractions from our real lives. If the media was not hypnotic, why is the television the first item we power when we enter the house? If the media could not brainwash a person, then why are advertisers using it to sell products? The television is the new God.

I remember when preachers in the 1980's called the television "a one-eyed devil." That phrase was used for years. I was young and did not realize all of the truth in that statement. I did not understand consequence when I was a young boy. I only heard the warnings in church. The more I grew, the more I understood what these preachers were saying. I still failed to understand consequence though. The one-eyed devil has a knack of interfering with the minds of men and women. It is referred to as the devil because it provides sinful ideas. The television promotes evil and makes violence appear normal. It is the devil because it becomes a medium between God and man. Whoever says that the TV is not dangerous is a liar.

I remember having a conversation with another man one day. The man said that the TV cannot make you do anything wrong. He said that the television cannot make a person commit a crime. He is stating a half-truth. The half-truths are the most dangerous, remember that. He stated something that can be believed. He stated something that can be defended in a court of law. The worst part is that he believed what he said. Men have a tendency to defend their vices.

I do it all the time. I find excuses to play video games. I find reasons to listen to old Wu-Tang Music. I need to let the hip-hop go. It is time to grow up. A grown man must let the kid stuff go. Entertainment can be an extreme waste of time.

The one-eyed devil can brainwash a man or a woman. The submission begins when the viewer powers the television. As soon as the television is turned on, the viewer begins to submit his or hers will to the message that is being delivered. This is a subconscious process. Once a man or woman sits in front of the tube; the brainwashing begins. Men, women, and children allow the media to alter their thinking without realizing it.

How many ideas are in your head now; that originated from the media? How many ideas do you accept that you know are wrong? You believe them anyway. How many activities do you engage in that you know are wrong? But you do it anyway. How many catch phrases do you speak that you received from television? You say these things all the time.

We are taught how to think by the media. We are taught how to dress from the media. We are taught how to practice religion from the media. Men are taught how to treat women from the media. Women are taught how to attract men from the media. Whether someone wants to admit it or not; we are taught how to respond to one another from popular media.

This media influence can be used for good. This media influence can also be used for bad. The good may be public education and sports entertainment. The bad is the subtle lies that are delivered through propaganda. One of the good messages I learned from the media is that America awards more social freedoms than other nations. That is a good thing. I would not want to live anywhere else on Earth in 2014. But I also adopted some terrible ideas from the media. One of those negative ideas caused me to be depressed and oppressed for years.

One of the worst ideas I extracted from media propaganda was the need to develop an ego. I had to prove to everyone that I am somebody. Most teenagers fight because of a demand for respect. We operate with the assumption that someone disrespected us. This is a lie. It sounds true but it is a lie. No one disrespected me. No one disrespected you. We just believe it happened.

The need to produce an ego is propelled by insisting that a person is lacking in some area of his or hers life. We lack respect for ourselves. The media is always creating thoughts of inferiority. Watching television will make a man or woman feel worthless in his or hers own life. I accepted the lie and attempted to concoct an ego. This led to a lot of trouble.

The media also teaches men to seek fame and fortune. This desire is not bad. The desire for fame and fortune is not necessarily an evil aspiration. I believe we all should seek credit for our work. We all should earn enough money to support our goals and dreams. The underlying message propagated by the media is to succeed at all costs. Whenever a famous person states that he or she will die for money, something is wrong. That type of speech should not be presented to children. Too many teenagers and young adults have ruined their lives believing that they should risk their lives for cash and attention.

I made many risky decisions because I thought I was supposed to. I made many risky decisions to build a reputation. Many of the men and women I surrounded myself with made hazardous decisions to earn money. Living for the moment was the mindset. I can only imagine how different my life would have been if my team and I planned for the future.

The truth is that my life is not bad now. I am not living in poverty now. But millions of men and women are in prison, dead, or living with disabilities because of the street life. We learned that way of thinking. We learned to lie, cheat, steal, rob, fight, and kill. The media immersed us in negative images and provided the soundtrack. The music videos arrest the imagination. There will always be a cost associated with telling young children how to think. No one can strangle the imagination year after year and not expect negative consequences.

The imagination of the children has been perverted and distorted by what they see on television. I have heard stories about incest. Anyone who believes the images on television are not reshaping the minds of children is lying. I never had that issue because I was immersed in philosophy, religion, and power. I also played a lot of sports. My interests in philosophy were distorted because of propaganda and negative church experiences.

The lesson I learned from the media is that it attacks what is already incomplete in a man or woman. A person who needs physical affection will have that need satisfied in an illegitimate manner. A person who needs power will achieve that need in an illegitimate manner. A person who needs love will fulfill that need in any form available. We have become consumers with little patience. I said it before; it is too easy to blame television for our social ills but movies and music help propel a weak person into severe self-destruction.

Hollywood lies to us. The movies were intended to be a reflection of the real world. At some indistinct point in time, the movies became the reality and man decided to reenact the movies. How did men become imitators of the movies? When did we decide that our lives were so meaningless that we began to act out our favorite characters role? The actors were supposed to be imitating us. Now we are imitating them.

Hollywood lied to the children and convinced them that they can sin with no consequence. I made many decisions and expected no punishment. The movies taught me to live my life any way I want to live my life. And eventually, I will get what I want because I am a good person. I wish that was true. Men get what they work for. Men get what they give. We all usually have what we truly desire in the end. But there are many years of pain and suffering in the middle. After the pain is gone; we still must deal with the scars and guilt. Regret is another factor that can cause a man to feel depression.

I always thought that I can be anything I wanted to be. I truly believed that lie. Everyone cannot be what they want to be. I would guess that 90% of the people in America are not what they want to be. That percentage is probably too low. Most men and women work jobs that are available. They are not working jobs that they want. The reality is that everyone cannot be what they want. Every 16 year old Black boy in America cannot be the next Black president. Every basketball player will not become an NBA player. When do we learn reality? When are we taught how to exist in reality?

I always wondered how the best athletes dropped out of school. I always wanted to know why the best athletes did not play ball for their high schools. Hollywood fills us with these dreams and we walk away hoping our dreams come true. But when the movie ends: life begins. The day by day struggle is impossible without a support system. The day by day fight is impossible to win without grace. The best athletes have the highest hopes. The higher the hope, the longer the fall.

Maybe we are afraid to succeed. Maybe the dream is too big. Or maybe we need the right people surrounding us. Hollywood is a major influence in our lives. I cannot blame a movie for the failures of a generation of criminals and drug addicts. But our culture allows the sitcoms and movies to play a large part in our lives. The propaganda and the fables we get from the media box leaves a major mark on our minds. I remember when I would say to myself, "I want it all or nothing!"

I let the hip-hop lifestyle cause me to lose a business opportunity. I was affiliated with a business man who started a cleaning service. I had an opportunity to help him start the company. I chose to go to a hip-hop showcase and perform. I convinced myself that I could get a record deal by performing at this showcase. I was living in Georgia during this time. I was caught up in the fast and flashy lifestyle. I turned down long-term security to take a chance at becoming a star overnight. What kind of person walks away from a secure business opportunity for a gamble at a hip-hop show? A man who believes that life has a quick fix button.

I went to this show and performed well. But I did not get any large recognition. At least 200 other emcees were there. Many of them had large catalogs. Many of them showed up with albums finished. I realized after the event was over that I probably should have followed through with the cleaning service. I missed out on that secure position because I was dreaming of a better life that only comes to a chosen few. I learned that day to stop gambling everything.

I adopted that irrational behavior because of my frustrations associated with working. I worked hard every day of my life. And I still felt broke. I was still living check to check. I was always being harassed by the police in the Atlanta area. I was just tired of it all. I wanted to believe that I could just become a rapper or a producer and not need to work anymore. I was hoping to get involved in music and be happy. I can happily sit in a music studio all day and night.

How many other men just get tired? How many men get tired and step out on frustration to commit a crime? How many men are in prison because of a robbery committed out of desperation? That man may not even be a true criminal. But he was desperate. Men make terrible choices because of desperation. Not because of evil. We know who the evil ones are.

Hollywood may not put the mask on our faces and load the pistols; but we get negative inspiration from the movies. We feel insignificant because we not famous. We feel like we are not getting what our God said we deserve. There must be something else for us. Where is our reward? If no one wants to give us our reward, we will just take something. We are takers. We become takers. It was not the original intent but after years of being taken advantage of, we seek to take advantage of someone else.

We see the famous people being rewarded with millions of dollars by acting like us. They get paid to act like us. We are hungry and tired from being ourselves. But we see these people in New York and Los Angeles becoming wealthy for portraying our lives. How do you think that makes us feel? Maybe we should define who the "us" is?

The "us" is not some angry Black men. The "us" are the men who do what they are supposed to do and life continues to be unfair. Some of us suffer from depression and bitterness. Some men can overcome the injustice. Some men cannot overcome the injustice. I have friends who work for fortune 500 companies. I have friends who were able to start their own businesses and thrive. I have friends who were never manipulated by the media.

Several factors are involved in the development of a man. Certain factors can break a man's will. Certain factors that break one man may strengthen another. Psychologists and criminologists conduct studies each year to determine the instigator of criminal behavior. The "us" that I am writing about are the men who get desperate. I am writing about the men like me. The ones who fell into the trap and allowed their gifts to be misused. I do not accept excuses but we can identify some. I have lived long enough to know that any man or woman in a desperate situation is capable of doing some insane, criminal acts. Do you think every stripper wants to strip? Or are these women in desperate need of easy cash?

I am providing a few more excuses for our wicked behavior. But it is a matter that must be explored. The lies we live with can make us ignore our faults. The lies we live with will further perpetuate the desperate lifestyle. Men will continue to be desperate and depressed. Women will continue to misuse their bodies and beauty for fast cash. The excuses must be identified and then taken away.

The Hollywood fantasy affects people in many different ways. One of the ways it affects people is spiritual. I already mentioned the cerebral aspect. We start to think differently. The spiritual aspect involves ego and morality. Hollywood invokes a low level of life. Hollywood desensitizes the masses. The vulgar language and the naked bodies produce an animalistic nature in the viewer.

A few years ago I noticed how comedians open their acts with a series of profane words. The cursing continues until the audience is dumbed down into a state of infancy. The vulgar opening removes reason and now the audience will laugh at anything. Movies also open the same way. A movie with no substance will start with sex, nudity, or a large amount of bloodshed. The audience is now ripe for downloading. The animal level allows the viewer to become a mind numb receiver. He or she will accept anything the performer says.

I know of successful and educated men and women who have world views that are distorted. Successful and educated does not mean whole or perfect. High class families suffer from the same conflicts the lower class families suffer from. I do not accept this as a coincidence. One would assume that the high class families are functioning at a greater level than the less fortunate. But this is not true.

What if the image of the great American family that is offered by the media is wrong? What if the lie offered by the media is causing the disorder among families. If every family is tormented with the same problems, something is wrong. The lies we live with cause us to reject the truth. It happens to us all. We try so hard to fit into a system that we may not belong in. our dreams and goals cost so much to achieve. Once we get to the level we wanted; we realize it is not what we need. It may even be unhealthy. But it cost so much, who has the strength to walk away?

What lies did you get from the media that you live with? Did you produce an alter ego to become a rapper? Are you playing a sport you hate because it brings you fame? Are you living the thug life because you see it in music videos? Are you a stripper because you too proud to work an ethical job? Why are you doing what you doing?

Maybe you were submissive in high school and college. You have the business and corporate job. Are you happy? Did you arrive? What is your definition of success? A friend of mine is playing professional football. He told me that he was jealous of my wife and three children. I told him I wish I was playing professional football. What is success? Do not let the media define success for you.

What I have learned in my few years on Earth is that the richest people are usually the ones who provide the best illusion. The people on television make a lot of money. The musicians, athletes, and politicians make a lot of money. The rest of us are spectators in their world. This bothered me when I lived in Georgia. I knew I could do more with my life.

I always felt like I deserved to be in the mix with the famous. I wrote better song lyrics. I had the ability to play sports. I also have a high IQ. I could not understand why I was not rich and famous. I was not the only man who felt that way. The city of Atlanta is filled with envy. Most large cities are filled with envy. A few rich and a lot of poor. This condition produces social unrest. A man would rather be an infamous gangster instead of a nobody.

We have dreams and fantasies implanted into our minds through verbal imagery and visual imagery. Those images produce concepts and ideologies. Those images form our world view. Hollywood will lie and sell you a dream that cannot be achieved. The music videos will showcase women that you may never date. The models in the videos will make a man lose interest in the real woman who loves him. The media must be reduced to a minor level of entertainment.

The present reality is that young men and young women are unsupervised. Young men and young women are skeptical about religion. Young men and young women are looking for leadership. These young men and young women search for idols and instructors. That search culminates on MTV and BET. The lost ones find their idols on the television. The visible music artists and athletes show tangible results from their work. The boys and girls looking for direction choose rappers and athletes as role models.

This would not be a negative choice if the boys and girls had men and women in their personal lives who can show them how to live a real life. Inspiration and ambition must be balanced in a child's life. We should not be living in a season where every boy wants to be a rapper or producer. We should not be in a nation where every girl wants to be a model or basketball player. Someone has to be normal.

The last statement I made feeds into the propaganda. How do we define normal? How does the media define normal? Is a doctor normal? Is becoming a lawyer or professor normal? How many high school students want to be cops or psychologists? What is a normal job? Can you live your whole life and not be famous? Is normal boring? Have you accepted the lie that a normal life is not exciting? What is normal?

I can mention a hundred Hollywood lies in this writing. I have seen a lot of movies in my life. I may write an entire book that is only about Hollywood. For now I will mention one more lie. This lie implies that a normal life is boring. Is a normal life boring? What is normal?

The normal life involves working an eight hour shift on a job and coming home each night to pay bills. That is the normal boring life. Wasting your life serving a company that does not care anything about you. That life is detested. Most factory workers hate their condition. Most office workers are not content with their situation. The high level supervisors are probably more satisfied than the lower level employees.

The normal life is a life of overtime and bills. The middle class families struggle with taxes and health care. These are the realities. How many children are actually excited to start a life that consists of nothing but bills, taxes, and medical expenses? Not many teenagers or young adults are happy to move into that season of life. That life is made to appear as mundane as stressful. The routine life of a person who works every day is stressful. But it is ultimately rewarding. Freedom is not free.

I remember when I moved into my first apartment. I worked every day and hated it. My cousin and I had to pay bills and go to work every day. If felt like a free prison. The street life felt so much better. The street life was exciting and dangerous. Those are the two tenets we were taught to seek. My friends and I wanted to live dangerously. We wanted to juggle different women and make fast money. The motto in 1997 was, "money, power, and respect." The normal life was boring.

I don't remember any conversations about marriage. Getting married was stupid. How can I be Hollywood if I have to worry about pleasing an unhappy woman? That was the image we saw. A submissive man, who never had any money, wasting his life attempting to please a woman who can never be satisfied. That was the media's portrayal of a marriage. Who would want that?

The lies we live with affect our perception of life. We can make decisions about our future based on an internal belief. I missed a business opportunity because deep down I thought I could sign a million dollar record deal. I let that fantasy cost me a job. (but what if I did get signed that day?) We ingest a lot of bad information while we watch television. We are bombarded with propaganda each hour we sit in front of the one-eyed devil. The television never shows us what the True and Living God desires of our lives. If we knew Him at an early age; we would be rescued from a lifetime of pain.

The truth is that family is good. Marriage is good. A man can be rescued from his own self-destruction if he has a wife at home with him. She will help him become the whole person God designed. The man will help the woman become the whole person she was designed to become. It is not about fame and fortune. It is about being whole on the inside. The man and woman who become whole internally will be an inspiration to everyone they come into contact with. Fame and fortune will then find them. Instead of moving to New York or Hollywood to be important, attention and resources will find you.

## PROPAGANDA

Propaganda comes in many different forms. Propaganda is a system of coercion that is designed to change the beliefs of the recipient. Propaganda is a subtle form of brainwashing. Propaganda is used by anyone and everyone. The practice of it is not inherently wrong. The practice of propaganda is neutral at its core. The person using propaganda may be good or bad. The words and images used to broadcast the propaganda may be good or bad.

What is propaganda? Propaganda is defined as a means of communication designed to influence the masses toward a particular belief system. Propaganda is designed to change a group of people's minds. The purpose may be political, educational, or economic. The intent of the message can be to improve lives or destroy lives. The ends may be beneficial to the ones sending the message but detrimental to the ones receiving the message.

Propaganda is used on a large scale. A large scale may be a presidential election. Propaganda may also be used on a small scale. A small scale would be an ad promoting lemonade in the summer time. Propaganda delivers a message to persuade people to change their behavior.

The lies we live with are sometimes provided for us through the media. A good lie that many of us accepted as true, through propaganda, is that athletes and celebrities are better than the rest of us. Another lie I hear often is about religion. Many of the social commentators believe that religion is not necessary. Christianity and Islam are attacked by the media on a daily basis. The media can shift a person's opinion with a movie. One magazine cover can change the way a teenager experiences the rest of his or hers life.

I remember the way I felt about sex after Magic Johnson made his announcement about HIV. That topic was discussed by several teachers at my school. I was walking through the hallways at Dozier Middle School feeling afraid to get close to loose girls. That announcement made my friends think before we engaged ourselves with other girls. Propaganda can be good. That announcement forced us to think about our actions.

A magazine cover can change the world. This is an uncomfortable truth we have to admit. I still remember looking at the cover of the *Source* magazine to see how I should dress for school. My generation used these visual images to define ourselves. We did not read *Black Enterprise* or the *Wall Street Journal*. I do not remember anyone exposing us to that world. It is unfortunate that we did not see that part of our society. I will expose my children to it now.

One magazine cover can change the world view of the masses. The styles that men and women adopt come from the media. When rappers were placed on magazine covers with sagging pants and covered in tattoos it was labeled offensive. After several years; those images became normal.

Now, in the year 2014, almost all of the teenagers and young adults wear their jeans or sweats below the waist. Many women are sagging their pants too. All of a sudden, women want to dress men. American society was publicly conservative in the past. The public has now adopted a behavior that is extremely liberal.

Men, women, and children are now decorating themselves in tattoos. Propaganda declared that this practice is acceptable. Visual imagery numbs the senses. An act that violated your conscience in the past because you were sensitive to it can pass by you and go unnoticed.

The ultimate goal of propaganda was stated by Edward Bernays almost 100 years ago. Edward Bernays stated that, "Men are rarely aware of the real reasons which motivate their actions." This statement reveals the true purpose of the media. Propaganda will have a person making decisions that he or she does not have an explanation for. Who controls your thoughts?

Why do you spend your money the way you do? How much money have you wasted? Is your life your own? I remember wasting years of my life attempting to be what others expected me to be. I remember not taking pictures for years because I did not recognize the man in the picture. I cannot explain this with any words. I just know how I did not see myself in the mirror. I would look in the mirror and see something man-made. What I should have been looking at was someone God made. That is peace. That is when a man experiences harmony within himself.

The propaganda is designed to control your impulses. Propaganda also implants desires. Propaganda will also compel you to follow the majority in your personal decisions. This happens in almost every institution within our culture. I remember when Gold was the primary type of jewelry worn by men and women. I had a few gold rings and gold chains. I moved to Georgia in 1998. All of a sudden I started seeing people wearing silver chains, silver bracelets, and sliver rings. I was not paying attention. Platinum jewelry became the new normal. Platinum jewelry was being endorsed by the hip-hop artists.

I was watching the movie Best Man with my wife. We went to the movie theater to watch this show. A pivotal line in the movie was spoken by the actor Morris Chestnut. Morris Chestnut made a statement about the wedding ring he bought for his fiancé. The statement he made was a bit of propaganda. His character said, "The ring is platinum, gold is played out." That is a perfect bit of marketing. I wish I had some stock in platinum that year. I can only imagine how much platinum jewelry was sold the year this movie was released.

When I heard that line; I immediately wanted to own some platinum. I had some gold but I never bought platinum before. I always felt that it looked too much like silver but it cost as much as gold. But that line made me want to buy some for my wife. I felt insecure for about five minutes. I had to remind myself it was a movie.

The truth is that we are all insecure about our lives. We feel this way because we assume the person next to us will judge us based on the popular trends. I wonder how many men and women felt anxious for not having any platinum after viewing that movie. If that movie did not make a person feel naked, I know that some music videos did. I know that music is just as hypnotic as a movie. People fight in nightclubs because of the message in the music. We feel like we have to prove something to the next man who is just as scared and insecure as you. We are really fighting ourselves. That is why no one wins.

Another popular form of propaganda is the need we have for more toys. The media is constantly bombarding us with commercials and billboards that compel us to consume. The media wants to separate us from our money. Propaganda separates men and women from their money by subtly suggesting that you need more. A good example is the lie we usually tell at night. The lie we all tell when we look in the refrigerator. How many times have you stood in front of the refrigerator and said, "There is nothing in here to eat"? We all do it. Propaganda wins again.

The ultimate goal of propaganda is to not only compel people to consume, but the ultimate goal is to implant the idea that you always need more. Once the idea is implanted and internalized, a mass of people are on autopilot. McDonalds can stop airing commercials today and families will still continue to eat there. The idea is already implanted. McDonalds is fast, fun, and convenient family food. And now McDonalds has their own generic version of Starbucks. The whole family wins. McDonald's advertisements make you feel like you are missing something when you drive by and don't stop in to eat. My children ask for it every time they see the Golden Arch. Preprogramming will leave a person on autopilot.

The white man is the devil. Black men are only good athletes or criminals. Men must keep the women happy or they will not be happy. I need a college education. These are forms of propaganda. Each statement is filled with prejudice and bias. None of these statements can be proven right or wrong. These ideas may appear harmless but each one impacts our lives. We begin receiving propaganda at birth. The average child sees 10,000 ads a year. That is a large amount of brainwashing. A child can be left on autopilot after a lifetime of sitting in front of television programming.

Propaganda is so strong, that it can ruin a family. We live with the lie that a happy home is not enough. We learn the lie that men cannot be monogamous. Women are taught that men always need a mistress on the side. Women are also taught that becoming a housewife is demeaning unless the husband is wealthy. Men and women are taught that marriage is an institution of bondage and misery. All lies.

The propaganda alters a man or woman's perception before the marriage. The propaganda produces a fear and anxiety before and during the marriage. The man and woman who choose to marry must address their premonitions as soon as possible. If not, their fears and worries may surface. Sometimes we manifest our fears and worries. What a person is afraid of comes to life. A marriage will be what a man or woman makes it.

We must not allow rumors, people's opinions, television programming or scenes from movies to determine how we operate our relationships. The messages I heard as a child made me not want to get married. When I did consider marriage, I searched for a perfection that is not attainable. When I finally did get married, I was still not satisfied. I was frustrated with myself and my wife. I wanted something that was impossible.

The influence of media on decision making is real. Anyone seeking marriage should first seek good counsel.

Seek the counsel of a couple who has been married over a decade, and nurtured healthy children. I would not get counsel from someone who has been divorced more than once. My opinion. I trust the husband who remained with his first wife. I know he sacrificed, loved, humbled himself, and prayed.

I have many more excuses for not beginning my marriage properly. I have many excuses for being incarcerated four times. I have excuses for not being wealthy and owning my own business. We all have excuses. How do we accept responsibility for what we did not know? But this book is not about excuses. I just want to identify outside influences. How many of us truly have original thought? Most of our identity was provided for us. Think about it. How much of you is original?

## MIS-EDUCATION

I wanted to add a chapter about the bad ideas we learn in school. I will mention a few of them here. I can probably write an entire book about the flaws in our public school. But I think we should not hate the public schools as a whole. We should take advantage of the free education. Whenever a flaw is identified, we should help resolve it.

I will identify some of the wrong ideas that are shared in public schools. These ideas come from adults and administrators who share their own personal experiences. Their ideas are not always wrong. But their ideas can produce dead ends and frustration. Every person cannot follow the same path and achieve success. My hope is for students and parents to understand how a half-truth can lead to pitfalls. Some half-truths are just lies told by good people with good intentions.

One of the lies I heard the most is about college. Every student does not need to attend college to improve his or hers lifestyle. College produces debt for the student and his or hers family. College produces extreme stress for the student and his or hers family. How many high school students are ready and prepared for the college and university life? College is not for everyone. Leaders and teachers should not make students feel that they will not achieve success without a college education.

I composed a short list of the millionaires and entrepreneurs who succeed without a college degree. The list is: Charles Culpeper, owner and CEO of Coca Cola; Dave Thomas, founder of Wendy's; Colonel Harlan Sanders, founder of Kentucky Fried Chicken; David Green, founder of Hobby Lobby; Annie Bieler, co-founder of Auntie Anne's Pretzels; Ansel Adams, world-famous photographer; Richard Branson, founder of Virgin Records; Simon Cowell, American Idol; Walt Disney; and Steve Madden. All of these millionaires followed their dreams. The pursuit of their dreams made them happy. Their happiness lead to their accumulation of wealth. The Bible states, "your treasure is where your heart is."

I remember the *Cosby Show* and *A Different World*. These two shows were very positive. These two shows promoted the need for higher education. I loved them. I loved their ideals. I sit with my three children now and watch reruns of the *Cosby Show* and *A Different World*. Both of these shows implanted the idea of college or nothing. I love it though. We should strive for more. I believe everyone can benefit from a higher education. I hope all three of my children strive for a higher level of learning after high school. But what if they don't?

Balance is essential to a healthy lifestyle. I remember the phrase, "Do not put all of your eggs in one basket." Attending a university or college is not the only path to success. Hundreds of millionaires never attended college. Hundreds of other entrepreneurs and millionaires dropped out of college when they discovered their passion. Balance in expectations is important.

Passion is important. I commend anyone who encourages students to seek a college experience. Especially the teenagers who only know their town or city. I would recommend college instead of the military. I believe the military has less freedom than college. A young man or a young woman may have a better military career if he or she attends college first. Just my opinion. I am an iconoclast. Children should develop their passions instead of learning facts. Adults should build new things and add value to an institution. There is no value in becoming a hired hand. Working a job without exploring your own passion will corrupt the soul.

A few other options are available to high school students after graduation. I learned of many options to self-improvement. Trade school is a good option. A man with a trade license can start his own contracting business. Trade schools offer carpentry, painting, plumbing, HVAC, and diesel mechanic classes. I was enrolled in a residential wiring class at one point. I considered becoming an electrician. Trade schools are a good option. A small business can be launched after earning a license in a specific skill. Which means independence must be learned.

Independence must be taught and learned in high school. I wish I was aware of the business opportunities earlier in life. I heard about owning a small business. But I never knew the first step. I had the mentality that I needed a million dollars first. I remember telling a friend that I would save a $100,000 from working throughout my lifetime and give it to my son when I die. I wanted to give my son a head start in becoming wealthy. This is still a good idea.

I would like to see a program that teaches children how to build small businesses and become leaders instead of workforce programs that teach servitude. I always tell my children to think independent and build something. All three of my children are using their innate gifts to see what their passions can produce. I am also showing them techniques and methods to earn money with their creations and ideas. We are getting an early start. I will not let them believe the myth of college only. I want them to know that they can produce income and opportunities on their own.

I just heard the story of a teenage girl who built a business out of recycled metal bottle caps. Anything is possible. This girl is still in middle school. She may not need college. When she does decide to go; a university will give her a scholarship. She will be attending college for free. Universities and colleges want iconoclasts and entrepreneurs to attend their schools.

Teach passion and not the memorization of facts. Human beings are not computers. We should not just teach kids how to accept our ideas. We should help them develop their own. I am a person who cannot be settled into one mode of thinking. I have a Master's Degree but I hate school.

My education did improve my lifestyle. I learned how to write papers and conduct efficient research. School also taught me how to think professional. I learned how to behave tactfully and express myself in the corporate setting. My passion for counseling, sports, and faith still needed to be appeased. I eventually realized how to blend my education with my passion. I used what l learned in school to print out Bible study lessons and organize a schedule to coach youth football. Education does help us.

The first time I went to college, I was 23 years old. I have no idea how I would have responded to college at 18. Let a child know that he or she can wait for college. Inform the children that they can make a final decision about their future at a later date. Every choice does not have a deadline. The concept of now is also a lie we live with each day. The Bible says the fruit that belongs to you will remain ripe on the tree until you ready for it. We all should stop rushing our plans.

The other main issue I have with the current education system is the debate about Creation. How do the public schools get permission to tell children that they were created through evolution? I can write about many issues with the Department of Education. But the teaching of evolution may be the most detrimental element of all. Why is this taught to children? It is a theory that has never been proven. It is a theory that was refuted by the one who created it.

When a teacher and a university professor tells a young man that he is a descendant of a monkey; how do you think he will respond to social pressure? He has no frame of reference.

Teaching a group of children that they came from bacteria and monkeys removes their awareness of the soul. If the children begin to believe that there is no God; they will not submit to anyone. If there is no God, then I can do anything I want to do. The goal is to evade detection of immoral deeds. The psychologists who spread the doctrine of evolution admit that their goal is to make room for human reason. If they allow God to be sovereign, then they would have to end some of their inhumane studies and controversial research.

This type of thinking is a response to cognitive dissonance. Psychologists cannot justify the large amounts of medication that they prescribe to patients if a God created us. Psychologists cannot justify the false diagnosis that they make on patients. The false diagnosis are used to bill insurance companies. The education system enables medical professionals to use patients as guinea pigs. The practice of medicine lacks proper discretion.

The need to remove God from the public and corporate conscience was spawned by greed and power. Money is what keeps the theory of evolution alive. Educational institutions must continue informing each generation that no God created us. Our souls are made up of chemicals, hormones, and emotions that need to be tamed with medicine and social programing.

Scientists, like Sigmund Freud, developed theories and explanations for the feeling of guilt and shame. Freud and many other psychologists attempted to discover physical and social variables that produce feelings of depression and anxiety. Instead of admitting that there is a universal law of right and wrong; the medical community would rather create its own rules. The rules they created allow them to experiment on children. The rules they created allow them to take advantage of uneducated women. They know humans did not evolve from apes. But they must keep the charade alive to justify their immoral deeds.

A scientist must remove the soul and the humanity of a person to make his or hers conscience comfortable with abortion. No mentally stable person can kill a baby, and sell its organs to science. The murder of a child is evil. But the theory of evolution allows for those types of "calculated" decisions. Science allows for measured and explained choices. Science allows men to be the measure of other men. When men begin to measure the decisions and actions of other men; right and wrong can be redefined. Without the Word of God. That is what the Book of Genesis described as "eating from the forbidden fruit."

Our public schools want to explain away God. My oldest son felt ashamed to carry his Bible to school. That should not happen. The removal of a God has caused children to live with no restraint. The lack of restraint has increased immorality. The lack of restraint has caused an increase in rebellion. Authority figures are not obeyed anymore. This is the result of reducing humans to talking animals.

The other symptom of this Godless education is the removal of gender distinction. Males and females are different. Males and females are different physically, biologically, emotionally, and mentally. Scientists and psychologists began rewriting their textbooks. Some of them want to continue with their experiments and explore theories. This will require the removal of gender.

The first step was the installing of unisex restrooms in public schools. The long-term effect of Sigmund Freud's plan to end shame.

Shame is essential. Pain is necessary. When people begin to live without shame; no rule will go unbroken. People without shame will embarrass themselves and their families. God implanted us with an anti-self-destruct mechanism. That mechanism can only function if we have fear, shame, guilt, and pain. The human heart must be soft and pliable. We cannot hear God if we become cold and fearless. There must be the opportunity of feeling remorse.

The emotions that I was taught to ignore were the very emotions I needed to change my life. I need to be weak to change. I need to be pliable and flexible to change. When I received that revelation; I immediately remembered when the world started teaching my friends and I to be hard. "You have to hard to survive in the streets!" That was a motto. That language was in the music.

My generation was built on being hard. Even the boys and girls who were not living the thug life wanted to be hard. The athletes wanted to be hard. The musicians wanted to be hard. The girls wanted to be hard and sexy at the same time. Hard was the way. We learned that behavior from the videos. We learned that behavior from the playground. Respect was earned by fighting. A boy had to be hard. The level of tenacity was based on which neighborhood you lived in. Hard was the way. Survival of the fittest. This was a good idea if it allowed young men to be supervised by the elders. But that does not happen in America. Our fathers are always working. I immediately recognized the internal conflict when I gave my life to God. I could not be hard anymore. This was a contradiction.

How do I live for God if I cannot be hardcore? Can I still be a man if I become soft? Will I lose my manhood if I become sensitive and timid? Will I be able to walk around campus as a sensitive saint? I will be ridiculed right? Manifesting the hardcore image is easier.

I mention this dichotomy of the hardcore, hip-hop image versus the kind and gentle image of a Christian saint. I had to deal with it on several occasions. I remember the confusing signals I emitted. Sometimes I did not know how to act. Act. That was the main issue. It is not an act. Living for God is a steady walk. It is a journey. Exhibiting courage is acceptable. God never made a weak man. The Bible allows a man to be a courageous, confident, strong person.

The irony of this piece of misinformation is that a child of God must be hard. He or she must possess a mental fortitude that can withstand ridicule and opposition. The child of God must possess enough strength to control his or hers emotions. More strength is needed to restrain oneself than is needed to lose control. Any three year old child can get upset and fight. But a mature teen can muster enough strength to restrain his or hers temper.

When I was in school a Muslim person was acceptable. Living as a Christian was unacceptable. I did not know why the culture accepted Muslims and not Christians back then. It still does not make sense to me as an adult. It is very imperative for children to have the right information early. Years of heartache will be avoided if the child who gives his or hers life to God is properly educated. Jesus is the real God. No disciple should be ashamed.

Why are the ones who subscribe to the Gospel of Jesus Christ ashamed? Maybe their education in religion is not right and exact. If Jesus is the only real God; there is nothing to be afraid of? The one who is following Jesus has the advantage. Somehow the world convinced Christians that they were weak. The fact is that the Saints are the victors.

## EDUCATION IN RELIGION

Education in religion is a subject that requires more attention. Education in religion is essential to spiritual and moral development. When I become aware of a new religion, I will research that religion. I will learn the origin of that religion. The origin of a religion will reveal its validity and purpose. Religious education is essential to understanding universal law. A proper education will expose propaganda.

Every man, woman, and child should learn the origin, purpose, and function of his or hers own religion. This applies to Hebrews, Christians, Israelites, Muslims, Jews, Catholics, and any other religion. The study of the origin, purpose, and function of your chosen religion will uncover truths that purify the soul.

True study will remove the façade and public image of a religion. Most cultures and religions are portrayed falsely through the media. The media never reveals the truth about an institution. The media only dispels myth and lies.

TBN is a Christian station that only promotes the worst representatives of Jesus Christ. I am convinced that most of the preachers on TBN never knew Jesus Christ. Just my opinion.

Scholarship is essential to spiritual growth. Only in the religious institutions; can a leader be a member for 20 years and still not know anything. Doctors, lawyers, athletic coaches, scientists, detectives, and military soldiers all grow each year. Why don't religious leaders grow? Why do I meet so many Christian men and women who cannot answer basic Bible questions? I believe one of the reasons American Christians appear foolish and fearful is because they do not have answers and knowledge of their own position. When I surrendered to God, I began an immediate search for all truth.

When I began my search for God, I studied many different cultures. I studied many different theologies and religions. I learned many different philosophies while studying various religions. One of the lies that is promoted through the media is the fable that all religions are the same. All religions are not the same.

The other lie that is told involves the identity of God. All religions do not worship the same God. Every God has a name. Every God has a purpose. Almost every God has a symbol that its followers observe. All religions do not worship the same God.

How many of you devote hours of your life to Bible studies? I have devoted years of my life to Bible study. The studies I engaged in as an adult answered the questions that I never had answered when I was a child. Studying is a good method of learning. Studying will allow a person to learn about religion, but he or she will also learn about his or herself. My studies revealed my own condition to me. Once I recognized my own issues, I was able to see how I can be a negative influence on the world. Once I recognized my own issues, I acknowledged the fact that I can be a positive influence on the world, too. Every man and every woman can be a positive of negative power in this world.

Bible study showed me what was wrong with me. The mass media has a tendency to transform men and women into judges and critics of the world. Our peers have a tendency to transform us into judges and critics of other people. My study of the Bible prevented me from becoming a judge and a critic. My studies compelled me to change myself. My studies showed me how awesome my Creator is. The studies showed me the Real Jesus Christ. The Real Jesus teaches his followers how to solve problems. The Real Jesus teaches his followers to heal themselves and teach others. I could not hide from truth when I discovered truth. Bible study uncovers truth.

Bible study also proved that God has a name. The True and Living God is name Jehovah. When we refer to Jehovah living in the flesh of a human body; we use the name Jesus. It is not true that every time someone uses the word

God; he or she is talking about the One Universal God. That is a lie. Many of the people on Earth have erected their own versions of God. The word God has many meanings. The one true God is Jesus/Jehovah. I learned that fact through years of study. I also learned that people do not study because they do not want to know the truth.

The truth about our culture is that people do not want to know truth. The truth will remove all excuses. Once a person learns truth, he or she cannot use a lack of knowledge as an excuse anymore. I learned so much truth in three years of study; that it started to scare me. I can honestly admit that I wanted to stop learning. I learned some truths that made me afraid to look back at my past. I began to erect walls around my mind. I began to learn extreme self-restraint.

Maybe I should write an entire book on truth. It is a good idea. Most of the men in the world do not know truth. I wonder if people want it. Do you want the truth?

The truth hurt me because many of my issues were caused by my own decisions. I made a lot of bad decisions. The Bible informs the reader that this world is full of traps. The Bible informs the reader that his or hers own wisdom will lead to hurt, harm, and danger. The Bible is the guide. God already warned men against making their own decisions. God already knew that men would find methods to ruin their lives. I had to learn to wait and pray. When I was a teenager, I made hundreds of bad decisions. I let my emotions dominate my reason. I let my anger and pride overrule my faith.

Jesus is called light. Jesus is referred to as light because light provides improved sight. Light provides vision for those who lack vision. Light reveals obstacles, traps, and enemies in hiding. Jesus protects, guides, and also leads his disciples. No other God is alive and living inside its Creation. Truth is, there is no other God. But that is another story. All of my studies proved that there is no other God. Jesus is the Light. What else do you need?

When I studied the other religions, I learned how human beings create new imaginary Gods. These new imaginary Gods fit the personal needs and selfish desires of the ones who created it. The people who lived off seafood created water Gods. The people who lived off the land, worship the trees and earth. The people who lived by the stars and signs in the sky; worship the sun, moon, and stars. Humans have always re-created God.

The need to create new Gods was spawned by the rebellion in the human heart. Instead of obeying the True God and allowing him to guide our steps; we would rather create other God's. By creating idol God's to worship, men can appease their spiritual needs while controlling his own steps. The false religions also allow religious men to control the spiritual growth of other men. But they can only control the people who don't study the concept of God for themselves.

Every man or woman is responsible for themselves. If we can study fashion and sports; we can study God, too. I have encountered many people who say that their pastor or spiritual guide never told them the truth. That is an excuse. The submission we are taught as children is a detriment to our lives. We live with the lie that a spiritual person must give us the truth. If the leader does not state a fact, it must not be true. It is amazing that people still wait for church to be told how to think. But we study music, sports, fashion, and secular philosophy every day. We learn millions of facts and ideas that do not profit our lives. Why not study the most important element of our lives? What is your relationship with God?

I follow Jesus. I was raised as a Christian. I was never fully persuaded that the Hebrew God was the one True God until after I studied other religions. I would advocate for all children to study alternate cultures and religions. I would allow children to learn various worldviews in a control, supervised environment. The best method of identifying truth is to measure it against opposing evidence. I talk to my children about other religions and opinions all the time. I want them to see the difference between the Bible way and the other way.

It is important for my children to know how others think. It is important for my children to be able to address lies, myths, and opposition. The only way to protect the mind is to study your own beliefs and have a decent understanding of the beliefs of others. This is most important in high school and college. The social studies courses contain lies and myths that affect the minds of growing children. The psychology classes teach worldviews that remove morals and values from society. I encountered some foolishness in college. I heard some of the most outrageous philosophies explained to me. I could not accept them because they made

Men the measure of man. This is a dangerous doctrine to obey. Men should never be the measure of man.

When human beings become the judge, jury, and punisher of men; we lose our power to be objective. If I am the judge of you, I will not condemn you for being just as wicked as me. I will ask you to join me in my deviance. If man becomes the measure of man, no one is wrong. I will incorporate my power to remove those who do not agree with me. There is no right or wrong. There is only: you against me. And the most powerful group wins. The group that achieves victory is not right or wrong; they are just in agreement with their ways and customs.

"Man is the measure of man." This theory is a lie. But many cultures espouse this theory. It is a theory that removes the True and Living God from His sovereign role. What God said about right and wrong is the measure of man. If God said the gay lifestyle is wrong, then it is wrong. If God said that tattoos and body piercing is a misuse of the human body then it is wrong. I was once a person who agreed that humans determined what is right and what is wrong. I no longer feel that way. I no longer believe that I, on my own, (with my own wisdom) can determine right from wrong.

I used to believe that a colony of people could decide amongst themselves what to think, feel and believe. I used to believe that people could agree on a set of rules and follow them together. I was once an idealistic person who had faith in humanity. I just knew that we could govern ourselves. It never happens. Life proved my myth to be wrong. Humans change their minds too often to settle on a strict set of rules. Humans cannot remain content forever.

The human heart is insatiable and unstable. The human mind is never satisfied with what it can see and understand. God implanted us with free will and imagination. These characteristics were intended to make us builders and explorers. These traits have been used for good and evil.

The lie associated with our ability to explore and build is liberty. I can do whatever I want to do. I can have whatever I want to have. I can take whatever I want to take. I may be able to write an entire book on liberty and the perversion of it. My first book scratched the surface of the deception of freedom. I have learned more about human nature since writing that book. Maybe I will write a volume two.

You cannot do whatever you want to do. All actions have consequences. None of our deeds are free. I am fully convinced that people rebel against God because they want to do their own thing. Men create their own plans and strategies. The internal conflict that arises from this rebellion must be explained away. This phenomena is the reason that religions develop their own understanding of simple Scriptures. Islam has three different mainline denominations.   Judaism   has   several   different denominations.   Christianity   has   22,000   different denominations. Cognitive dissonance again.

Some of the revisions to the meaning of scripture were produced to support immoral behavior. Governments in several nations create amendments according to their needs. These nations use spiritual sources as inspiration to justify their actions. A lot of nations do this. Religion is used to protect the government from its wrong doing. The religious leaders are the middle men. Citizens are subdued by the spiritual leaders. Whenever a civil unrest is building; the priests, preachers, and elders stop it. The governments continue abusing their power as long as the churches protect them.

An example is in India. The government uses the spiritual law of Karma to explain poverty. Indian citizens are not permitted to feed the poor good food. The public view is that Karma is the reason they are poor. The poor are suffering because of evil in their past lives. This is a misuse of a false doctrine. Can it get any worse than that? The misuse of a false doctrine.

Another good example of this was the establishment of America. A group of explorers invaded this continent and made it their own. A group of natives were already here living and worshiping their God. A new group arrived by boat and murdered them. These people created a religion and government that fostered ideology to support their killing and oppression. The lie we were told in school was based on freedom. The Europeans arrived in America to practice the freedom of religion. But they destroyed the Natives ability to practice their religion on their own land.

This group also taught their ideologies to the next generation. The Europeans children continued to oppress the Natives children; who were here first. Those ideologies are based on lies. Their lies produced massacres, lynching, murder, and racism. Jesus said, "You will know them by their fruit." Jesus never told anyone to rob, steal, kill, and murder for his gospel. The Bible said that the devil will steal, kill, and destroy. That means the people who stole the land from the Natives are devils. That means the Indians in India who starve the poor because of Karma are devils. That means the Catholics who murdered millions to control their land and resources are devils. The definition Jesus defined is the description of the enemy of our souls.

Who steals, kills, and destroys in the name of God? No Hebrew would ever do that. But some people call themselves American Christians and support the negative ideology. There is nothing honorable about the way the Europeans destroyed the Natives and continue to imprison them on reservations and in penitentiaries. There is nothing honorable about the constant revisions of history that attempt to explain the genocide.

Those lies are now a part of the history and education of America. An old saying is "Tell the lie enough times, and it will become the truth!" Education in religion has enabled me to understand world history. Studying religion has enabled me to understand world government. It almost appears that each nation's government is provided a religion to maintain its social order.

Each religion is used to control the people in that nation. Without that nation's primary religion oppressing the mind of the followers; the people would probably revolt. But when a religion is designed to produce guilt and role playing; the people concede to it. When Christianity became a religion that uses God to obtain material wealth and fame; it attracted all the wrong people. This is what I see happening.

I meet hundreds of people who hate Christians because they believe that the White people who stole North America from the Natives were followers of Jesus Christ. The people who believe that also blame White Christians for the destruction and oppression that is taking place in Africa. The African continent contains thousands of different minerals. Those minerals are used by other countries to manufacture high-tech products. This stealing and raping of the land is blamed on White Christians. It is sad that a religion is hated because of the actions of wealthy corporations.

Jesus should not be hated because of the actions of Europeans. But He is. I meet Black people every week who reject the True God because of the past actions of White people. I also meet Black people who follow Jesus because of their position given to them by White people. A form of Christianity was created by our technologies and institutions. America has Bible colleges and Bible conferences. Anyone can conveniently live the life of a disciple but not be a true disciple. In other countries, Christians with Bibles are murdered. How many of us can survive that life? Im just saying.

I will write about that idea at a later date. But I do have one question. What would happen if no music was played in church? More than one question. What would happen to the Christian Hip-Hop artists if no music was allowed in church? Would they still be committed religious people if there was no stage? What if there were no gospel choirs? How many young people would attend church? I just wonder how much church would exist without the choirs and rappers. How many men and women would be happy with their form of Christianity if they did not have these titles?

I can rap but I never do it in church. I can be a producer but why should I? There is a lack of Biblical education available to people. The knowledge of God is needed to free people. I need the Biblical scholarship to remain in a whole marriage. I need all the wisdom from the Bible to nurture and educate my three children.

Almost everyone I encounter is an evangelist, prophet, prophetess, teacher, preacher, pastor, bishop, Dr. reverend, or apostle. It is sad. But the streets are still full of blood and sin. I respect the men and women who are in the streets and hospitals. I respect the volunteers I see at the prisons. We must do the work. Not have a title and find places to speak what was learned in the classroom. We must live the life of a disciple and go to work. Any imposter can perform on a stage. Any impostor can go to a Bible school and learn about a God. How many can actually live it. I was placed in positions that forced me to live the life.

It is true that the Natives of North America were slaughtered and oppressed. It is true that Africans are enslaved in their own land. But it is not true that Jesus is to blame. It is not true that the followers of Jesus Christ committed these acts. The myth is that the Bible was taught to the slaves and natives to make them compliant in their own destruction. The lie is that Christianity is always taught to undermine the victims will. This is sad. But I believed it once upon a time.

I can be labeled a Christian. That label is used to describe countless groups of people who claim Jesus to be a great prophet. The Christian label is used to compartmentalize everyone who declares right from wrong. I do follow Jesus but I use the term with reservation when I am in a public place with strangers. I am careful because of the misunderstanding of the word. I do not want to be prejudged before I have the opportunity to develop a relationship with others. The real followers of Jesus did not harm anyone. But the label places us in harm's way.

Sometimes I do not use that label. I consider who I am having the conversation with before I decide to label myself. The term Christian does not have the same meaning in every social circle. I have been hated by people I never met before; just for using that term. When I ask about the animosity; the other person shares a negative past experience with me. This type of incident has repeated itself over and over again. I am always apologizing for the actions of others. The idea that all Christians are the same is a lie. The idea that all Christian beliefs are the same is a misunderstanding.

The various groups that are mistaken for Christians do not follow Jesus Christ. The Mormons are mistaken for real Christians. The truth is that the Mormons do not worship the same God of the Hebrew Bible. The Mormons worship something else. The Mormon God is a plurality of beings. The Mormons believe that men can become God after death. The truth is that the Hebrew Scriptures state there is only one God. Jesus Christ.

The Catholics claim to be Christians. Anyone who conducts a study of the Catholic catechism will discover that the Roman Catholic Church does not worship the True God of the Hebrew Bible. The Roman Catholics worship their own version of a God. The Catholic catechism contains a proclamation of faith that states followers will become like God. CCC. 460 is a section of the Catholic catechism that states, "For the Son of God became man so that we_might become God." "The only-begotten Son of God, wanting to make us sharers in his divinity, assumed our nature, so that he, made man, might make men gods." Faithful Catholic priests and spiritual leaders believe that they will become equal to God. This is wrong thinking. This false doctrine also contradicts the Hebrew Scriptures.

The third religious organization that masquerades as true Christianity according to the Bible is the Church of Christ Scientists. The Church of Christ Scientists do not worship the God of the Hebrew Scriptures. The doctrine that they profess is an antichrist doctrine. I was confused about it at one point in my life. I meet other people who do not know what the Church of Christ Scientists represents. The doctrine of the Scientists is the complete opposite of what the Hebrew Scriptures teach.

I researched the doctrine of the Scientists. Their interpretation of the Scriptures is distorted. This method of altering the real Scriptures allow them to manipulate the facts about God. Men have always wanted to use the power of God. Men have always wanted to control or govern the knowledge of God. The Christ Scientists pervert the Word of God to empower themselves. The woman who started the cult wanted to eliminate right and wrong. Her goal was creating a religion that allows man to measure man.

A few of the heretical concepts espoused by the Scientists are as follows. The Christ Scientists believe God is a power that cannot indwell man. This is a lie. The Scientists believe that God is the mind in Man. This is a lie. The Scientists believe that Jesus Christ is an idea. This is a lie. They also believe that the Christian concept of the Trinity is a form of polytheism. This is not true. The Father, Son, and Holy Ghost is one God who operated in different functions to achieve His goals. Another element in their doctrine denigrates the position of Jesus Christ. The Scientists claim that Jesus did not pay the penalty for sin. And they teach that Jesus is not God in the flesh. Any religion that denigrates Jesus Christ is wrong.

There are a few more elements to the Christ Scientists that must be exposed. I see these elements as detrimental to soul. Everyone must avoid this cult. One of the elements is the fact that Christ Scientists do not believe that a devil exists. Humans do have a spiritual enemy. Regardless of the name we give that enemy; we do have an enemy. Another element that damages a person's spiritual condition is theory that evil and good are not real. The Scientists teach this lie to their congregation. This doctrine allows people to live with very little guilt.

The other theory that the Scientists live by is their belief that matter, sin, and sickness are illusions. This allows the followers of Christ Scientists to absolve themselves of any reason to submit to God. If nothing is real. I can do whatever I want to do. This agrees with the doctrine of Aleister Crowley, "Do what thou wilt, is the whole of the law." Aleister Crowley was a confessed devil worshiper. Christ Scientists are living the antichrist existence.

I can also mention how Islam is a counterfeit religion. Islam is considered an Arab and African religion. Islam is accepted by Black people in urban areas. Islam is also accepted in the correctional system. This religion is accepted by those who do not study without opposition. But Christianity is opposed by those who study and those who don't study. Why?

We live with lies. The lies are implanted into our minds while we are infants. We ingest these falsehoods without resistance because they were introduced while our minds were most pliable. The other major factor that allows us to accept falsehood is the degree of trust for the messenger. Many of my Muslim influences in life came through Black men. I had very little trouble trusting Black men. I was raised a Christian but I always had reservations.

Islam was introduced to me in several different forms. I was introduced to the Nation of Islam through Malcolm X. I learned about the 5% Nation of Gods and

Earths through the hip-hop music. I was also taught the Orthodox form of Islam as a teenager. These three versions of Islam are all different. The Nation of Islam, 5% Nation, and Orthodox Muslims are not one in the same. Some of the terms that they speak with are similar.

Some of the language that the members speak with is the same. But each religion is separate and distinct. They all use the word Allah, but they are not identical. Just like the Christians, Mormons, and Catholics are not identical.

No one should accept the lie that all religions are equal. The only Muslims who can enter Saudi Arabia are the Orthodox Muslims and the well-versed NOI members. I mean well-versed because an American Muslim must be aware of the strict customs in Saudi Arabia. The 5% percenter cannot enter Saudi Arabia. The 5% Muslim cannot become a member at a Mosque unless he adopts the true tenets of Orthodox Islam. They are not the same. The Orthodox Muslim will be willing to teach the 5% Muslim.

Recruiting is always a tool used by Orthodox Muslims. Islam is the fastest growing religion on Earth.

Islam, Judaism, Catholicism, and Christianity are not the same. I see the COEXIST bumper sticker on cars. I see the COEXIST shirts worn in public. It is possible to coexist with various religions. Just do not make the mistake of assuming each culture is equal. All of the various religions do not share the same worldview. The Christians, Jews, Hebrews, Muslims and the cults are all different.

I read the Holy Quran. Their teachings do incorporate the killing of those who are not Muslim. The Muslim writings do state that the Holy War involves killing everyone who rejects their religion. The Jews are killing the Arabs on the land that they stole from the Arabs. The Catholic Church has been killing people on various continents for hundreds of years. The Mormons killed hundreds of people as they spread across America. All of the forefathers and spiritual leaders who established these religions used murder, intimidation, and extortion to spread the message. Only the True Hebrews who followed Jesus Christ spread the message without violence or intimidation. The 12 apostles never killed anyone.

The 12 apostles never hurt or harmed anyone when they traveled through Africa and the Middle East sharing the gospel of Jesus Christ. The only force they implemented was the Word of God and the gifts of the Spirit. Jesus told the disciples we will not live by the sword. Jesus wanted his true followers to know that if they used physical force to share the message; it would not be based on grace, internal peace, and God's sovereignty.

Salvation is a free gift. Salvation cannot be coerced or forced onto a person. Salvation cannot be brainwashed into a person. Salvation cannot be based on memorization, ceremony, indoctrination, or emotion. The Lord Jesus Christ indwells his creation. Jesus alters the heart and mind himself.

Truth is, we have nothing to do with salvation. Jesus does it all. Truth.

The lie. We can change God's word and get the same result. The truth is that we must avoid sin and rebellion. Jesus already knows what each of us needs to be in harmony with Him. Jesus is the Way, the Truth, and the Life. There is no other method of living that is better than His way. The reason we have so much strife is because so many people have developed so many different ways of living. Each way only works if the leaders can produce servants.

The constant need for servants destroys the humanity in people. The culture produced by the false religions and the distorted true message corrupts humanity. The leaders become Gods and followers become peasants. God intended for us all to be on a level playing field. Perfect equality is not possible but at least God made a culture that allowed everyone to share and contribute. God's way prevents the destruction of dignity and honor. God's way also prevents men and women from becoming too powerful. The Bible states that the greatest among you is the servant of everyone. The human philosophy changed that model. Our way is totally opposite. The greatest among us has the most servants. That's wrong.

An example of how we distorted the model is witnessed in government, sports, church, and education. Why are athletes paid more than school teachers? Why are government officials making millions of dollars on the stock market and not assisting their constituents? Why are preachers earning millions of dollars and still accepting offerings and money from poor people? Why are the citizens, parishioners, and students allowing these unfair actions to happen? Why?

The people who submit to these unbalanced cultures are people who were taught to obey orders. We live in a world that produces a submissive population. People do not question their position in life. The people who do question their roles, positions, and condition are labeled rebels. The people who do question leadership are labeled disobedient. I had to sit in the hallway at my high school because I told the science teacher that God created man. The teacher wanted us to accept the theory of evolution.

I still remember that week like it was yesterday. I was so disappointed in my classmates. None of them stood against the teacher with me. None of them were willing to tell the teacher it was wrong to teach that theory. I was told that my religious view was not necessary in school. This was stupid to me because I was not a professing Christian at this time. I did attend church but I was not some religious zealot. Why is the belief in God creating man a religious belief? Who created that lie? Believing that a God created everything we see is not religious. It is truth.

Injustice continues and miseducation continues because people are taught to submit to authority; even when it is wrong. This type of mental conditioning is wicked. A man, woman, or child should always have the opportunity to think and ask questions. When a person loses his or hers liberty to ask questions, that person loses a piece of humanity. That person becomes a submissive follower. The person who stops asking questions loses his or hers willpower. That person will do anything everyone is doing the docile follower will believe what everyone else believes. The freethinker does not get along with the submissive follower. The two are polar opposites.

The educational system in America produces children who will ingest any idea that the government wants to distribute. School teachers are compelled to stick to their curriculum. Some of the religious systems will produce preachers who teach only what they are told to preach. Every denomination has its own particular agenda. The obedient ministers are elected to positions. These ministers can only teach what they are told to teach. They must be obedient, even if it is wrong. Attending public school every day can lead to a lack of willpower. God gave humans free thought. No one has the right to take free thought away.

What is a man who cannot think for himself? What is a woman who cannot determine right from wrong? Could they be zombies? Could this be the reason for the recent fascination with zombies in the media and movies? I don't know but I do know that men must think for themselves. Question everything. Pray for wisdom. Do what is right. Search for God. Judge people by their fruit. And then analyze the results of all your decisions. There is the answer. No lie.

## MAN

What is a man? What is the definition of a man? What lies are promoted to describe a man? What is a man? Can you think of any single words that label a man? Now a more difficult question arises. Where are the Real men? I hear that question a lot. I see that posted on Facebook constantly. Where are the Real men? So how do we define a man? What is a Real man? I think it is sad that these questions are asked in the year 2016.

How does the human race exist for 6000 recorded years and not know what a man is? I think we do know. But people do not want to admit that they know. If men and women admit that they know the true answer; they would all have to submit to a Real God. There is no man without a God. There is a no Real man without a relationship to a Real God. So, what is a man?

A man is a creature created by a God who is intelligent. The creation itself is perfect. God gave the creation the ability to think on its own. As the creation began to think, God himself implanted instructions to prevent the creation from self-destructing. The more intelligent the creation became, the more rules and boundaries God developed. The more man learned, the more God had to restrain him. God has always implemented boundaries to ensure the existence of His creation. Without God's boundaries, humans would have ceased to exist thousands of years ago. I have no problem with God. I have no problem with this definition of man. It really is this simple.

This is the simplest definition of a man. I will add a small chapter on the woman. Just to balance the writing. I am a strong believer that God wanted perpetual balance on Earth. He did not create women just to bear children. God is not a pragmatic being like men. Humans create machines and tools for one single purpose. But God provided identity and significance to all of His creatures. Nothing natural on Earth was created without significance.

Every animal, insect, and sea creature have a function and identity. Crabs, lobster, and oysters are water filters. Squirrels spread and plant seeds for trees and plants to grow. Insects and rodents remove disease from the Earth. God did not waste anything. If every animal and insect has a job and function, men and women are far more important.

What is a man? A man is a fighter, father, thinker, and worker. We were all farmers, hunters, and fishermen when we lived solely off the land. Our current high-tech system has removed some of us from the land and sea. Some men are now working indoors and on computers. The shift in vocation does not change the function of a man. We have just changed the method in earning wages. Men still fight, think, and work. We will always be competitive. Men will always think, reason, and have faith. Men will always work on something.

The father concept is an easy one to understand. Every man has someone who looks up to him. Every man looks up to another man. This is natural. I want to believe God implanted this desire. I always had a man that I watched. Some men I watched from a distance. Some men I walked under their wings. I always had a big brother. I had one biological brother. I also had brothers in my neighborhood. When I was in church as a child; there were men in there who I listened to and idolized. I call this the father complex because we always want a father and we want to be a father. Some may use the term mentor. This innate desire is one that cannot be ignored. This need manifests in all situations. Good or bad.

I cannot rationalize the fatherless children in this world. I cannot understand it. I never could understand the way a man could abandon his children. It is something that is unnatural. A mind must be destroyed and depressed to cause a man to abandon his children. A man has violated his purpose when he does not nurture, teach, and guide his children. I find it more ironic that these same men join gangs and raise someone else's child through it. He is still a father. But he is misusing the function. Why are there so many homes without a father? Why are so many women living together with their children? Something is wrong.

What is a man? I find my answers in the Bible. Once I learned to read the Bible as an instruction manual, and not a book of Good White Magic, I was able to find answers. The Bible is the man's instruction manual. The popular anagram is B.I.B.L.E: Basic Instructions Before Leaving Earth. I love the Bible. I see the history of men in the Bible. The Bible shows us the life and times of the ones who followed God and the ones who did not follow God. The past never lies to us. History repeats itself. The life of King David is a warning and lesson to us all. The Hebrews had the truth. The Israelites were closer to God than any other nation.

God chose the Israelites. God protected the Israelites. This Earth is full of people who chose not to obey God. The ones who choose to obey are persecuted by the ones who choose not to obey. So it is imperative that men obey God. Why? Because God fights for his people. I would rather be on God's team and have his protection than to be on the enemy's team and become God's enemy. So what is a man? You can be God's son or God's enemy. Choose a side.

All men must choose a side. We do not have the option of resting in the middle. God breathed breathe into us when we were created. There is no way to be separate from the presence of God. Every human is either an enemy or child of God. This is a truth regardless of a personal view of religion. This is a truth whether a person is religious or not. Human beings cannot be separated from the presence of God. Our conscience is the proof of this.

We all feel guilt, shame, and pain when sin is committed. That is the reason for the high dose of medication our nation is addicted to. Almost every child and adult is medicated. That medication may be prescribed pills or alcohol. Others medicate with controlled substances like marijuana. The fact is our guilt, shame, and pain cannot be ignored. God's presence is in us and always near. There is no escape. Some individuals are so distraught they choose suicide. That is a mistake because death will send your soul directly into the presence of God. Absent from the body means present before God. Now the final judgment begins. Who is ready for that? Who is prepared for the final judgement?

What lie are you living with? What lie have you accepted about men? Do you think men are thugs? Do you think men are perverts? Do you think men are misogynistic? Are men just pigs and self-centered? Do all men watch pornography? Is porn a symbol of masculinity? Is it mandatory to have strippers at a bachelor's party? Do all men cheat on their wives? Why? Where does this attitude come from? Why is sex always the measure of a man's self-control or status?

What other prejudices do you harbor in your mind concerning men? Are all men dogs? Is that true? Can't trust a man! All they do is lie. Really, is that true? What else have you heard? Niggas is crazy! (I will write a book on propaganda, this is the ultimate propaganda, we have these phrases repeated in so many media outlets that it becomes an automatic response. I can write a whole book just on this one phrase.

These three words are filling up prisons and cemeteries. These three words have become a mantra that curse Black boys who adopt it and a curse to the Black boys who don't adopt it. The good ones are considered fake and soft. The bad ones are worshipped for being real and hard... [Russell Wilson vs. Michael Vick], not fair but its real). My favorite is this following one. A real man is a thug and a gentleman. My favorite lie. I tried to live this one. I wanted men to think I was hard, and strong; and I wanted women to think I was fun and romantic. Tough balance, but I strived for it. Then the revelation came. I will explain that revelation in this chapter.

Are all of these statements lies? Are any of them true? Judge for yourself. Which one are you? Women, which one of these statements do you accept as true? What type of men do you socialize with? More importantly, how do you speak of men in the presence of children? We all must control our tongues in the presence of the children. Children are listening to every word we speak.

My sons will view women according to what I say about them. My sons will honor women the way I honor their mother. My daughter will view men the way my wife views me. My daughter will treat men the way my wife treats me. No one lives on an island. Every action and word is monitored by the children and heard by God. We must do better. And we must protect our children from the propaganda.

I will share the revelation I received about manhood. I will share how I was exposed as a fraud. I will share how free I became when the fraud was exposed. I am now free. I already wrote about the deception of freedom. I wrote about the way a person feels free but he or she is really enslaved to an idea. And as long as he or she is surrounded by others who accept the lie; the façade can continue. Well, God himself freed me from the façade. People can only help you if they are free. People can only help those that want it. Sometimes men get comfortable living wrong. Then we deny the help by denying we need the assistance. Sound familiar? Women do it too.

The phrase that I wanted to live by was used in several songs. I heard the statement used in several movies. It has been paraphrased in many different forms. This image has been characterized in many different movies. I see it in Black characters and White characters. The gangster and the gentleman. The statement is based on a duality of traits. The thug and the gentlemen. This applied to my personal life. I wanted to be good and bad at the same time.

My revelation concerning this image I wanted to uphold revealed how propaganda and peer pressure forced me to be fake. Propaganda removes the will to be an individual. Propaganda causes peer pressure. Just to prove it; where did the gangster and the gentleman come from? Why did I have to be one or the other? Second thought, what defines a gangster? What is the definition of a gentleman? The one who provides the term is the one who controls you. The one who provides the definition controls you.

This is the same peer pressure that compels college students to join Greek fraternities. The peer pressure causes feelings of insignificance and low self-esteem. Students just want to fit in. Truth is you don't need a fraternity or sorority to be special. Why would you allow a group to dehumanize you, embarrass you, shame you, violate you, and brand you before you join? That is called witchcraft. That topic is an idea I will explore later.

The gangster and the gentleman. The revelation forced me to think. I wanted to live up to someone else's definition of a gangster to prove I was a man. Their definition of a gangster does not agree with God's definition of manhood. I had to think about my life. I had to reconsider my actions. The whole process I used to become what I thought was a man was wrong. I was actually in a state of malfunction. Maybe that is why I stayed high and drunk. No man can successfully live in a state of malfunction. I wanted to be a gangster and still be good. It is not possible without persecution.

The opposing personality would also arise within me. The gentleman wanted to express himself. A gentleman can appear harmless. The gentleman is accepted in most social circles. The gentleman can get away with murder because of his manners and charm. The negative aspect of me wanting to become a gentleman is the rules of society that govern the behavior of a gentleman. It can only be an act. It is wrong to be wholly good and caring. That sounds like an obvious contradiction, doesn't it? But it is not a contradiction.

Every woman has a story of how kind a man was in the beginning. Every woman can describe a man who was sweet, romantic, gentle, understanding, and sympathetic in the beginning. But after dating for weeks or months, he became a dog. After a season, that man became violent, rude, obnoxious, and disrespectful. The truth is that he was always imperfect. The truth is that he was acting like a gentleman is expected to act. He was acting. Key word is act. He was not allowed to show his true self.

I can write a book on this subject too. But that will be in a book on dating. I am discussing the social norms that produce fake men and fake women. We live with the lie that a man should be a thug and a gentleman. But the truth is that the propaganda, peer pressure, and expectations associated with manhood cripple men. How do I become real in a fake world? The only answer is to be in communion with God. That would require a man to be a praying man. That would require a man to be a disciple of Jesus Christ.

The gentleman has a struggle. The struggle is his desire to be a good person without surrendering to a good God. The more the gentleman wants to behave well; the more he resembles the image Jesus Christ has set for him. The better he becomes; the more he recognizes the image Christ has set before him. The more the gentleman exhibits kindness, love, proper manners, and courtesy; the more he identifies with the image Jesus set before him. That is the point of discomfort. How can I look like Jesus and be me? Where is my identity? That is the issue.

The challenge of being a gangster is the school system, the workplace, and the police. How can a man be a true gangster and go to school? How can a man be a true gangster and get a job? The image of the thug versus the real one causes conflict. The conflict is increased when a man wants to be real about his acting.

This conflict becomes extreme if he joins a gang. The gang will have expectations for him. How does he perform his illegal work and still maintain his own identity? The gang immerses its members into a spiritual bondage. The only way to join a gang is with a demonic blood oath.

This pressure causes internal conflict. This pressure causes mental issues. How can I be a real gangster if I know it is wrong? How can I claim to hate White people and then get a job working for them? How can I be a thug and attend school? Shouldn't I be fighting the teachers and attacking the security guard? What should I be doing? I don't know.

The thug life and the gang life produces friction with family members. I behave one way outside the home but a different way in the home. More internal stress is created to overburden the mind.

If I stay a gentleman, I might end up in church. If I act like a gentleman part-time and a thug part time; I risk becoming bipolar. If I fake both images, I will please everybody. But now I am fake. What is the end result of this person's life? Stay tuned. You may know people living this bipolar life. Just watch them.

I tried to fake both images. The sad fact is that I did not realize I was faking both images. I was so good at it. When a man is living in rebellion to God and in rebellion to himself, he does not recognize it. A good word to describe this condition is delusion. I was delusional. Imitating others empowered the delusion.

I searched the television to find a good identity to emulate. Every man I knew in the 1990's watched Rap City. No one should find their identity through the media. No one should feel so insignificant that he or she cannot be satisfied with their own God created identity.

Once upon a time I mimicked my favorite rapper. I dressed like him. I talked like him. I even learned how to rap with his style. I ignored my real life and emulated his life. This is not an uncommon act. Most men and women are emulating someone else. Just look at the style of dress. Just look at the style of hair women wear. The increase in tattoos and the patterns of behavior show imitation.

When I received the revelation of how men mimic other men; I have had the ability to recognize this behavior in other people. Who are you becoming? Are your thoughts your own thoughts?

This is not just some social phenomena among Black men who watch rap videos. This happens in other ethnic groups. This happens in other cultures. White men imitate Johnny Cash, Eminem, and Kid Rock. Italians imitate Italian mobsters. Whoever denies their true identity that God gave them will adopt another identity that they received from this world. Any alternate identity is not your true identity. If you ignore your true identity self-destruction is coming your way.

Manhood is the issue. Authentic manhood was the goal. A man is supposed to have a job. But can a gangster work at a fast food restaurant? Can I be a thug and get all A's on my report card? I don't know. What type of thug can I become? Should I emulate the wild Jamaicans that are portrayed on TV? Should I be a blood thirsty killer like Al Capone? What do we do? Can a man follow the law and still be street? By the way, who makes the rules?

The one who makes the rules controls the game.

I had these issues. The revelation showed me how fake it all was. I was amazed at how fake the so-called gangsters were when I was in the streets. I knew some real ones. But the majority were fake. Their thug life was just an image. Most of the people living the life adopted it to fit in a group. Some of them were only involved because of fear. The real ones took advantage of the fake ones. There were a lot more fake ones. Some of the guys in the streets were there because they didn't want to work. Every man in the streets is not hard. Some of them were just sorry men. Men who were weak and did not want to work. As soon as they were arrested, they told on their partners. I was not surprised by the large amount of snitches. The ones who snitched were the fake ones.

I was even more startled when I realized the girls knew the boys were fake. The girls joined in with the fantasy. They needed the fake thug to promote themselves to the status of a thug princess. They were both fake and they both knew it. The girls were snitching every time they were caught committing crime just like the boys. The fake girls needed the fake thugs to fulfill their fantasy. The goal was to feel like someone of significance. If we both could be notorious, it was better than being forgotten. Role playing has ruined millions of lives. Do not live a lie.

I had some associates in my city who lived the street life 100%. They went all in with the culture. Only a few of them graduated high school. Most of them went to prison. A few are dead. The men and women who were committed to illegal money walked with a different spirit. They knew their lives would be short and tumultuous.

I thank God I did not die when I was making illegal money. When I realized how much vanity was in the illegal life; I just decided to make quiet money. I chose to remain low key and earn some fast cash. I never told anyone what I was doing. It was always friends who robbed their friends. Why should I get robbed and killed for proving I am real to other fake people?

The thug life was a fantasy that eased the conscience. The fantasy lasts until you get arrested. Young Black children emulate images we see on television. We imitate what we see and hear. We learn to imitate whatever excites other people. Children are good observers and good listeners.

The current trend of cross-dressing is an example of mimicking TV. Children have been watching their parents laugh at Madea for 15 years. Now the boys are dressing like women and behaving like women just to get laughs and attention. This needs to end. Do not teach children that the television is more vital to life than the real world.

We all need to unplug our televisions for a year. I promise the world would change instantly.

The gay man is now acceptable to the world. The gay man is unacceptable to God. The homosexual life is unacceptable to me. It is a form of malfunction. This alternate lifestyle was frowned upon until the media attempted to make it appear normal. We must hate what God hates.

Who do you agree with? No man would dishonor his body by engaging in intimacy with another man. Any man engaging in that lifestyle must be born again. He must be filled with the Holy Spirit. Only Jesus can change a man from the inside out. Some lines should never be crossed.

This lifestyle is the opposite of how God designed men to live. Living this lifestyle is rebellion against God and an act of self-hatred. You cannot oppose God without hating oneself. Our actions are symptoms of an inner conflict.

This matrix was the result of attempting to live a life without God. Men and women will always substitute their lack of harmony with God with a superficial image and superficial relationships on Earth. We have this need to feel like somebody. You are somebody when you are in communion with God. It is ironic because all of our insatiable desires can be resolved with Jesus. It is ironic how we long to be immortal and powerful, but we ignore the one source that can provide immortality and power.

The rise of social media has proven that humans need to belong to something bigger and wider than themselves.

Every human is born with a need to become transcendent. Transcendence only comes through a relationship with God. Social media has become the substitute for the transcendent relationship men should be engaged in with God. Men, women, and children connect with people from all over the world through social media. It only takes one second to have my thoughts spread across the whole world.

Transcendent relationships are used to replace prayer. Men use to pray. Men use to share their thoughts and feelings with God or family. Now I can share my thoughts and feelings with thousands of people at the push of a button. These people cannot help you. You are a sick person crying for attention from other sick people.

Nothing in life changes until a sick person cries for attention from a healer. The Healer is Jesus Christ.

I will not allow wireless technology to replace my relationship with God. I see the dangers of it. I have felt the pride and pseudo fame that comes from one of my posts receiving a lot of attention. The new technology is a gift and a curse. It will make a person believe that he or she is important. In reality, that person is not important at all.

A transcendent relationship is necessary to live a life of fulfillment. The Hebrew men in the Bible understood that fundamental desire. The men in the Bible always mentioned God and their need for His approval. Men join various organizations to be a part of something bigger than themselves. This desire to be transcendent is not always negative. This desire is similar to other elements in our lives. Everything God gave us can be used for good or bad.

There is an enormous amount of peer pressure in church. Who truly wants to be a virgin for God? That is a huge challenge for men. I had to struggle with sexual temptation as a teenager. It was hard because most of the teenagers at my church were not virgins. Several teenagers were having children while we still in high school. My faith was in constant chaos. I was in the wrong church.

Another internal conflict may be the athlete versus the scholar. The lie is that these roles are oppositional. Unfortunately, sports is viewed as a method used to prove ones manhood. Why can't scholarship be viewed as a form of exhibiting manhood? A father may force his son to play sports to prove how tough he is because good grades are not enough. I remember believing there is nothing masculine about reading books. Another stereotype.

I had to live this out to see its profound impact on my life. I can now see how the stereotype affects my two sons. My sons must decide between living a holy life before God or accepting their roles as lady pleasers. My sons must decide if they want to serve God or use their natural abilities to serve themselves.

They are natural athletes. An enormous amount of attention comes with that role. A lot of power and respect comes with that role. I see how they are pressured to respond and act in a preconceived way. Black boys are expected to act a certain way according to their gifts.

I speak about this topic the most because I had to live through it. My wife told me that she was interested in me when we met because I was half wise and half street. She loved the fact that I could act like a bad boy and have spiritual conversations. The gangster and the gentleman.

I admonish the reader to explore his or hers own life. What image have you adopted? What stereotype are you living out? Are you living the life God designed for you? I finally began living the proper life at 29 years old. I hope you can identify your true identity earlier than I did.

A good method to measure your character and discover what lie dominates your walk through life is to identify your role models. What do you worship? Who do you worship? You will become what you behold the most. The person you worship will be the person you become. This may sound good but you will hate your true identity and hide

it. Hiding your own light from yourself is Antichrist.

## WOMAN

What is a woman? What are the lies associated with it? I admit I don't have all the answers. But I can offer some insight from a man's point of view. Sometimes we need the vision of others to see what is wrong with ourselves.

This is a sensitive topic. I am not a woman. I am not the most qualified person to discuss the proper identity of a woman. What I can do is use my knowledge that I acquired from my wife. I can offer the wisdom I am developing while raising my daughter.

What is a woman? What does a man expect from a woman? Are men and women different? What lie is associated with womanhood? I know some of the stereotypes. I hear the pleas women have in their hearts. I talk to women who need spiritual advice and emotional support. My wife and I have counseled women on several occasions. I hope I can help someone.

What is a woman? A woman is a precious and sensitive vessel. A woman is something to be cherished and honored. A woman is sacred. A woman should be treated as an exclusive item. A woman is different from a man. She must not be regarded as a man. A woman may share a couple of characteristics with a man. But she is still entirely different.

A woman was called a man's help meet in the Bible. The man was created first. The woman was formed second. The concept of the woman as a helper is a topic that prideful people debate. I never argue with the Bible. God chose our roles.

I do not believe God wanted women to live as slaves to men. A help meet should not be viewed as a subordinate figure. I can explain this positioning model with a familiar sports reference.

Michael Jordan and Scottie Pippen were perfect partners. Both men were valuable. Both had a specific function. Jordan was always viewed as the number one leader. Pippen was always viewed as the number two position. Neither man was more valuable than the other. Both of them were necessary to achieve success. Together, they were unstoppable. One man and one woman working together are designed to be unstoppable.

The similarities between men and women are based on our relationship with God. A woman is designed to be in communion with God. Just like a man. Women need men to complete their identity on Earth. And, yes, men need women to complete their identity on Earth. God has prescribed the method from the beginning of Creation. We need each other.

The other similarity between men and women involves fellowship. Men and women have the need to belong. Men and women join clubs, gangs, churches, lodges, and institutions. Men and women both play sports for the challenge and camaraderie.

The other similarities are based on the hierarchy of needs. Men and women are similar when they both assimilate into the American culture. Both genders are introduced to myths, lies, religion, and insecurities. Both genders are indoctrinated into a philosophy of inadequacy.

These four factors produce a man and a woman who needs the following factors in his or hers life: love, entertainment, fellowship, and drama. There is no coincidence that men need the same four factors to be whole. These four factors are basic human needs. The challenge is satisfying these areas in a positive manner. The consumer culture of America creates a status quo of inadequacy. The disposition of inadequacy creates tension within the man and woman even before they become intimate.

The Bible states that the woman is precious. Precious suggests that women must be treated as a special item. A woman is precious. It is not a secret that women are intoxicating to men. They must be honored and cherished the same way a man washes and waxes his car. I am not comparing a woman to a car. But sometimes men give more attention to dead objects than they give to a living woman. I still remember the stories I heard about men playing video games all night instead of engaging in conversation with their wife. How does that happen? An electronic device cannot return love.

How much love does a woman need? As much as a man can deliver.

How do dead objects get more affection from a man than a living woman? I wonder if women begin to feel inferior to the material possessions of men. I wonder if a wife ever feels like a man's possession and not his human partner. I still remember when my wife told me I treat her like one of my male friends. She was insinuating that I don't cherish her like a precious gift from God. I probably didn't. I had no idea how to be married. No one taught me.

Entertainment is an aspect of life that consumes time, energy, money, and resources. Entertainment is a priority to men and women. It is a major aspect of American life. This nation is so prosperous that we immerse ourselves in entertainment and still feel bored when it is over. The need for entertainment is caused by a severe anxiety. That anxiety causes an extreme desire for comfort.

Women seek this entertainment and comfort. This desire can cause conflict in relationships. Men want to earn more money with our spare time, but the women want comfort and entertainment in their spare time. This subject can lead to minor or major issues.

I will offer one example. Valentine's Day is a holiday designed to spoil a mate. Men do not care if we get any gifts. But women expect some great things. Just know, it is a lie if you believe that your husband or boyfriend does not love you if he does not care about this holiday. Pay attention to what he provides all year. Money, muscle, support, prayer, a good father etc..

This scenario is played out in thousands of other situations. The man is compelled to spend money he does not want to spend because he feels the need to entertain his woman. I lost women in the past because I would not spend large amounts of money to entertain them. I was criticized for not buying expensive clothes to impress women. (It was ironic because I would hundreds of dollars in my pocket and not tell the women I was with I had it. I just wanted to see the condition of her heart.)

Do women truly need material items to be satisfied? Do you really? Can a man with no money satisfy a woman? He should be given a chance. Social pressure is real.

I learned of a new phenomenon. Women are marrying men who are currently in prison. I find this new trend to be intriguing. I want to know what is causing women to marry a man she cannot physically be with instead of the free men in the community. How does a woman find more joy in marrying a prisoner than marrying a man who is not in prison? Maybe there is a high associated with the longing for him to be released. I am just guessing.

Is this type of relationship a mission to prove loyalty? I wonder if a woman would do this because of a desire to experience misery. The answer will always be love. So what is love? Does love require that you suffer alone? Does love require a woman to be unhappy before she can experience joy? The answer is no. Love does not require a woman to experience misery and loneliness first.

What is a woman? Is a woman defined by her pain? The media would make you believe that. There is a prevalent notion that women love negative drama. The female reality shows are full of failed relationships and fights. Thousands of movies show unhappy women who are defined by loss, tragedy, and suffering. For some reason, the woman who experiences the most loss, tragedy, and suffering is respected the most. For some reason, the media and the movies show animosity towards the woman who has avoided loss, tragedy, and suffering. The character who has the perfect marriage is ignored and considered inexperienced. This is backwards. The person with the perfect marriage is the one who has the perfect wisdom. This woman should not be ignored.

True wisdom is avoiding the negative situations. Show some honor and reverence towards the people who avoid pain and divorce. Maybe they know something the rest of us do not know. We have a habit of showing envy and hate for the people who enjoy good lives. Men and women hate people who don't make their mistakes. We then pride ourselves in surviving the negative consequences of our own decisions. This is sad but true.

Men and women both celebrate growing up poor. Women celebrate living as single mothers. Why? Women should start honoring the women who don't have children outside of marriage. Let us all begin to celebrate virginity and strong marriages. Honor the good.

So what is a real, honorable woman like? What definition do we use? Do we use the White American image of a woman that was promoted on television? The image of the Stepford wife. Do we honor the sexy Black woman who dresses half-naked? Who is the real woman?

A Stepford wife is a woman who was viewed as acceptable because she was her husband's servant. The Stepford wife had no mind or thoughts of her own. Her purpose was to serve her husband. This role was adopted by millions of families. Black and White families used this model. This is not God's design though. A woman must have control of her own. Mind a woman must be able to think for herself.

Would a real, honorable woman dress half-naked and call herself a classy lady? Should we place women who use sex as a weapon on a pedestal? What does God think of women who use sex as a weapon? Just because a woman can use her body to make money does not mean it is right.

What other definitions explain the role of a woman? I can write about dozens of them. I will focus on the ones that impact the lives of me and the people I know. I will not write about the Geisha girls in Japan. They don't have a major role in American culture. I will not write about the Muslim women in America. I don't know enough Orthodox Muslims to speak on their position. I do know Black women. I do know White women. I also know how the media profiles the woman. I read the negative messages the media publishes to cause women to feel weak and insufficient. Even when nothing is wrong with them.

A question everyone should answer is this. Are families following the media's model of a woman? Or is the media imitating the world? Judge for yourself. Answer this question too. Is your family following Gods' model for a woman? Or are you producing women the way you want them to be?

A common model of a woman we all see is the sassy, proud, Black woman. This is the image used in most of the movies produced by Black producers. The woman with the sarcastic mouth and the independent spirit is portrayed way too much by the media. I see it imitated in the community.

These images pollute the minds of young girls who think it is good. Pride is never good. A young girl must understand that rolling her neck and insulting people will eventually harm her. The independent spirit denies its need for guidance. Do not lie to young girls and tell them their sassy behavior is sexy and empowering.

There is nothing positive about the independent, prideful image. It is the opposite of the Stepford wife. I understand why the concept was developed. A woman wants to establish some sense of power and individuality. I understand how a Black woman may want to overcome her fear and nervous behavior.

I am learning how to monitor my own daughter. She has a sarcastic mouth. Little girls get away with their defiance and disrespect because they are cute. This may cause the behavior to remain.

I speak on this issue because it has become the stereotype for Black women. I get upset with the public expectation people have for Black women. My wife was accused of being dumb and weak because she is not sassy and proud. Other Black women have criticized her for being humble. She has to explain herself to other women; whenever she obeys me and does not do what she wants to do. Why does a woman have to explain submission to her husband?

The irony is that the women who question my wife have failed marriages and unstable relationships. Maybe my wife can teach them, instead of them corrupting my wife.

According to the Bible, a woman is expected to submit to her husband. The man is the authority figure of the family. The woman is the man's partner in leadership. Only one of them can be number one. This concept actually gives the woman freedom.

Freedom is more significant than the power pride desires to obtain. A woman should not strive to overpower her man. The man submits to God. All of his decisions will be judged by God. The woman can assist the man and maintain her mental freedom. Her freedom will enable her to focus on prayer and nurturing the children. If she obtains absolute power, she loses that freedom and now becomes loaded with responsibility. God established our positions for a specific reason. Trust his design.

My wife had to deal with this peer pressure because of the public stereotype of Black women. She is supposed to be a Boss. She is supposed to rule me. No, that is too much responsibility for a woman. Pray for the men. Nurse the men.

Educate the children. Heal the children. The children are killing each other and the rest are dying because the women are attacking the men. They were taught to destroy their men. The men are weak and dying because their original doctors and nurses have become their opponent. It is sad.

The lies we live with. The lies are destroying the family. What is a woman's role? Her role is to be her husband's help meet. That is not a role of servitude. It is a role of self-preservation. If the man maintains his power, health, and might; the wife will live a life of prosperity. Spiritual, mental, and physical prosperity. But if the woman has a sick, unhealthy, weak man; she will be depressed and burdened. Which one is better?

I could explore this concept a lot more. It is something that can be explained in further detail with family or marriage counseling. A woman should not feel insignificant or insecure by trusting a man for leadership. Allow the man to do the heavy work. Let the man make the difficult decisions. He will pray for wisdom and his family will win. Every man I know wants a woman who can help and support his work. Men work for the family. Everyone wins.

The example I used is referring to the prideful woman. I know a couple that consists of a powerful man and a powerful woman. They are both operating at their top capacity. But they have no children. There is a difference. They both support each other. But they have no children. They are married with very little distractions. Know your role. Identify priorities. Do not watch television if you want to be happy.

I also know of couples that have a woman on a mission. And the man supports the woman. That is a good model if both members understand their goals. The role of the man and woman must be defined. But nothing is defined if the woman has that proud, independent spirit. There must be good teamwork, transparency and open communication.

Unfortunately, that proud and independent spirit is the one promoted more than anything else.

The family structure has deteriorated in the world. The children are suffering because of the lack of proper family structure. It is not the woman's fault alone. It is the lies we live with. Men have some wrong ideas too.

The world and its propaganda has women focusing on things that mean nothing. I believe it starts with vanity. If the world can convince a woman that she is ugly or weak, the brainwashing can begin with no restraint.

Who told White women to compete with Black women? Who told Black women they need straight hair? Who told White women to cover themselves in makeup? Why is plastic surgery becoming the normal treatment? The newest trend I noticed is self-justification.

Self-justification is a new trend that I am witnessing among women. Skinny women feel a need to justify their bodies. Fat women feel a need to prove that fat is fine. I see

BBW online and on posters now. Why? Dark skin women want to prove that their skin does not degrade them. This need to justify oneself is the symptom of a bigger issue.

The bigger issue is media and propaganda. The media is designed to produce the spirit of inadequacy and insignificance. Do not watch television if you have any negative feelings about yourself. Don't watch it anyway. Women are under constant attack because of their image. It is not fair. Corporations can only make money if they can convince you that you are lacking; and have a need for their product.

It is not the men who degrade the women. Men are not as particular as the magazines claim we are. Men do not care as much about image as we care about maintaining peace in the home. The image does not outweigh the spirit. Peace of mind is important for men and women. The next time you see an ugly woman with a handsome man, realize she is a good person who produces joy in the home.

A man would be satisfied with peace in the home from any woman; as long as she healthy. You cannot be overweight and unhealthy. There must be some self-respect and maintenance. By the way, love is also prevention. If you love your family you will prevent disease. Self-respect will compel a woman to improve what can be improved.

Self-respect is vital to a woman becoming what God designed her to be. Work on your character. Self-respect will prevent hurt, harm, and danger. I know that a woman who respects herself will not have sex with men she is not married to. The woman who is mentally stable does not need sport sex. She seeks to maintain her steady mind.

The women who share their bodies with different men have the most psychological problems. This is a scientific fact and a spiritual truth. The lack of restraint makes a woman available for others to damage her. A man cannot hurt you if you don't allow him. I never met a virgin that contemplated suicide. The virgin understands value.

The value system that is instilled in a woman must be evaluated. How do you value yourself? I had a discussion with a woman last week. She compared herself to a female celebrity that is a known groupie. This woman said she felt bad because she never dated a rich man. Why would a woman compare herself to another woman who makes sex tapes? How can you envy a woman who is famous for her sexual prowess? A woman with honor should never compare herself to a stripper. The Bible labels that woman a whore. You must value yourself above a famous whore. This woman is dominated by inadequate thoughts and ideas.

The woman who does not value herself above the whore has some internal issues that must be addressed. Only a whore that does not get rewarded for her sin can envy a famous whore who is earning money and receive fame for immoral behavior. If this is the case, then the sexual immorality must stop.

I have never envied a male stripper. That is not a lifestyle I can participate in. I have never envied the fame and wealth of a male stripper. I know that lifestyle has its own challenges and rewards. I was not designed for that function. I don't compare myself with those men. So why would a woman compare herself to something she was never designed to become?

Women must compare themselves to God's image of a woman. What did God design you to become? Answer that question.

Women are not connecting with good men because they are not prepared to attract him. A woman in the wrong state of mind will ignore the good man in her life and avail herself to the bad man. The bad man allows the unstable woman to feel normal in her condition. A good man will cause the unstable woman to see fault in herself.

A woman in her wrong state of mind may become lesbian. This can only happen after depression and pride fortifies itself in her mind. In order for a person to commit to a life of perversion, he or she must be spiritually broken. That person must be spiritually healed.

A woman can only be prepared to receive what her mentality can maintain. Change the heart, change the mind, change the vision. A good woman will connect with a good man. She will be prepared to share, submit, and empower that good man.

The lie says that a woman must go to the club and dress seductive to attract a good man. This idea is also applied to church. The idea is that the more men you attract, the better the odds are one of those men will be good.

Another lie women believe is that she can engage with a bad man and make him good. A woman cannot change a man. The condition you accept him in; will be the condition he remains in. If he was a dog when you met him, he will remain a dog. Only God can change a man. But God must also perfect the woman.

What is a woman supposed to do to find a good man? Can she find a good man in church? Can she find a good man at work or in the gym? I don't know. The churches are becoming less and less about Jesus Christ. The church is not the holy place it used to be. The gym is a better place to meet a mate than the night club. Dating a coworker is dangerous for too many reasons.

My advice for any woman is to fix yourself. Get alone with God. The truth is a person is their own worst enemy. Spend a year praying and reading the Bible. Unplug the television. Turn off social media. Do this for a year. At the end of the year, you will be a different person. You will become a new woman.

A year without social media and television will also remove negative friends from your life. The lie is that we need wireless communication. You really don't. We survived for 6,000 years without it. This new woman will be able to communicate with men in a much better manner.

Now you are prepared to live the life God expects you to live.

I am learning and adjusting my worldview as my daughter continues to grow. I learn something new each day living with my wife. I can share ideas on worth, value, dignity, and pride. But the root to development is faith, temperance, and value. Without faith, a woman will never trust a man and humble herself. Without God, a woman cannot become her true self or help her man become noble and whole.

PSALM 86:11

Teach me Your way, O Lord; I will walk in Your truth;

Unite my heart to fear Your name. (NKJV)

## SOUL

All men, women, and children have a soul. The soul is our connection to God. The soul contains the mind, will, and emotions. We must not pollute the soul. We must not ignore the soul. Science teachers and professors do not want to acknowledge the existence of the soul. The admission that a soul exists would prove that a God exists. If God exists, the practice and study of science would be forced to change.

Do not accept the lie that humans have no soul. Do not allow science to suggest that there is no God. The evidence of the soul is present in our actions, emotions, and thoughts. The soul is what keeps us awake at night. The soul is the energy we feel emitting itself from the people we come into contact with. A simple hand shake can reveal the condition of another person's soul.

The soul connects us to the source of life. Without the soul, a human will be no different than an animal. I have met people who were so corrupt that I could not fellowship with them. It is hard to imagine that a human can become so dark that their words are dead.

I know many people who exist in that state. I know men and women whose eyes have no light in them. That state of existence always begins with pain and depression. This dark state is the result of sin, depression, abuse, and pain. We should avoid sinking into a dark state. And we must not mistreat others. The people we mistreat may sink into that dark state.

The soul must be protected. The soul must remain pure. The soul is immortal. The soul can be forever good or forever evil. Do not allow any outside influence to damage your soul.

It is the soul that contains our personality and identity. The body is not your personality and identity. How a person looks on the outside does not reveal his or hers soul. The true identity of a person is the condition of his or hers soul. The body responds to the will of a man. Our physical bodies are responsible for pieces of our personality.

The personality is partially developed by our physical bodies because people treat us a particular way based on our visible characteristics. It is impossible to ignore this truth. No two humans are treated the same. Skin color, head size, hair styles, and body shape dictate how a person will respond to you.

Short men are not valued the same way tall men are valued. Spanish men are treated differently than White men. A light skinned Black man is not feared the same way a dark skinned Black man is feared. Sad truths. I learned this lesson early in life. I was constantly told that I was better than my brother because my skin color was lighter than his. That was a lie. Skin color does not determine who is more valuable in a family.

Our personalities are developed by our encounters with other people. Our encounters are influenced by our physical characteristics. Our physical characteristics become our most dominant component in life. This can be a mistake. This can be an advantage too.

The mistake is produced if a child becomes prideful because he has more muscles than his friends. The muscle does not make him wise. He must not substitute muscle for wisdom. The other mistake is the woman who has a body that is shaped better than other women her age. Women begin to exalt themselves for the wrong reason. Do not substitute curves for dignity and honor. An exotic dancer will never get the same honor and respect as Claire Huxtable.

The advantage that physical characteristics produce for the soul involve vocation and corporate value. Some men will not make it to college without an athletic scholarship. Some women need sports to feel comfortable in their bodies. I felt strong and important when I played football. The brotherhood motivated me.

Our world is preoccupied with the flesh. We must not forsake the spiritual aspect of life.

Never consume more hours of the day concerned with physical features than the soul. More time and energy must be directed toward the soul. Prayer is more important than cosmetics. You should study the Bible and exercise. A healthy body with a corrupt spirit will not profit you. A lot of beautiful women are without a happy husband and hate themselves. The increase in cosmetic surgery proves that. A lot of handsome and healthy men are in prison. They were dissatisfied with their decent lives. A corrupt spirit and a polluted soul will ruin your life; one way or another.

My soul was on fire for years. I knew a God was out there. I knew right from wrong. I just could not function with a religion. I had trouble with the rules and I did not know the Bible. It is more important to know God and the Bible instead of surrendering to the indoctrination of a religion. The pressures of life will overcome a religious belief. But the pressure of life will not overcome the knowledge of the Word of God and a relationship with Him. The soul will be preserved and reinforced by the Word of God and communion.

Science is used to explain emotions, addictions, mental disorders, and destructive behaviors. The Bible explains these four facets of life as decisions and the results of our decisions. People make wrong decisions that impact their lives and the lives of others. Just like a person can make a positive decision that affects the lives of others. Our lives are all based on someone's decision.

The lie is that life is a series of random and unexplained events. This idea is not a lie. But this idea denies personal responsibility. This example is a sensitive one. Hurricane Katrina was caused by the Earth producing a storm. The people who died were the ones who did not leave when the warning was issued. The storm was random, but the choice not to leave was a personal decision.

The other belief is that God controlled everything that has ever happened. This belief is held by most religious people. God did not control everything that ever happened. God did not allow women to be raped and assaulted. God had nothing to do with that. God does not permit the child abuse and child sex slavery to exist. God wants it to end. But men must accept the challenge to stop it.

I am a man of faith and reason. God never intended for us to live without human responsibility. He also expects his creation to think for itself. If a man or woman has faith, then he or she must take risks to change the world. None of this will happen if the soul is buried by the flesh. A person who loves their image and body will never take a risk to stop evil. And that is not God's fault.

I view the world as half of God's providence and half of man's choices. I see my current life as a result of my own decisions and God's grace. My life is a result of my good and bad decisions. But my life is also a series of moments

God himself orchestrated to produce a result. The Bible shows us how men make decisions without considering all the outcomes. God himself has to intervene to prevent one person from destroying every life that he comes into contact with. If we operate with the assumption that God does everything; then men and women would not be responsible for their sin, rebellion, and mistakes. There is a mysterious balance to all of this.

Our souls must remain clean. Our minds must remain positive and untainted. Our deeds must be performed with the right motives. It is very easy to lose our innocence. The world makes sin appear normal. The world makes perversion appear acceptable. We must not adopt the world's view of right and wrong. I always ask myself the same question when I have a decision to make. My question is, "What did God say about it?"

An easy method to judge your influences is this. Ask your spiritual leader three questions. "What is your view on sex? What is your view on money? What is your view on power?" The answer to these three questions will reveal your spiritual leaders true agenda.

God's answer is the truth. Men will adjust the truth to fit their lifestyles. What lies are you living with?

This is just the beginning.. more volumes on this subject are coming.

AND YOU SHALL KNOW THE TRUTH,

AND THE TRUTH WILL MAKE YOU FREE!!

What lies are you living with?

Which one describes your condition………..

I am _____ .

I think that _____ .

I could never_____ .

People think I _____ .

My father said_____ .

My mother said_____ .

But I _____ .

My family never_____ .

I could never get married because_____ .

Black people are_____ .

White people are_____ .

Money will make me _____ .

I think God is _____ .

Heaven and Hell is _____ .

College is _____ .

I don't think I will ever be _____ .

I just provided a few excuses that hold us back.

Pray and then write down the wrong ideas trapped in your mind.

Identify your mental condition and analyze the root of your thought process. How do you think?

Write down all of your own superstitions.

Write down the misconceptions you have about the world.

Write down the negative ideas you have that came from external sources.

Then write down every time you self-destructed when you had the opportunity to succeed.

Just keep writing, writing is therapeutic.

I may do a second book on this topic. I only scratched the surface.

We kill ourselves ladies and gentlemen. The devil can't do it. God made us too strong. We ingest one wrong idea and then begin to kill ourselves.

It's time to fix ourselves and ask God for help.  PEACE!!

The following pages are quotes from the past about truth. I read dozens of books. I study random topics to enhance my life and the life of the ones I come into contact with. Enjoy. Only one of these quotes is mine.

## Quotes about the truth

In a time of universal deceit - telling the truth is a revolutionary act.

### *George Orwell*

I am a firm believer in the people. If given the truth, they can be depended upon to meet any national crisis. The great point is to bring them the real facts.

### *Abraham Lincoln*

All truth passes through three stages. First, it is ridiculed. Second, it is violently opposed. Third, it is accepted as being self-evident.

### *Arthur Schopenhauer*

I'm for truth, no matter who tells it. I'm for justice, no matter who it's for or against.

### *Malcolm X*

Man is least himself when he talks in his own person. Give him a mask, and he will tell you the truth.

### *Oscar Wilde*

Truth is a deep kindness that teaches us to be content in our everyday life and share with the people the same happiness.

### *Khalil Gibran*

Tell the children the truth.

### *Bob Marley*

The truth will set you free, but first it will make you miserable.

### *James A. Garfield*

I am the Way, the Truth, and the Life. No one comes to the Father except through me.

### *Jesus Christ*

If I'd written all the truth I knew for the past ten years; about 600 people - including me - would be rotting in prison cells from Rio to Seattle today. Absolute truth is a very rare and dangerous commodity in the context of professional journalism.

### *Hunter S. Thompson*

There are some people so addicted to exaggeration that they can't tell the truth without lying.

### Josh Billings

Truth exists; only lies are invented.

### Georges Braque

There is no greatness where there is no simplicity, goodness, and truth.

### Leo Tolstoy

Adversity is the first path to truth.

### Lord Byron

The first reaction to truth is hatred.

### Tertullian

The pursuit of truth and beauty is a sphere of activity in which we are permitted to remain children all our lives.

### Albert Einstein

A lie told often enough becomes the truth.

### Vladimir Lenin

Despite my firm convictions, I have always been a man who tries to face facts, and to accept the reality of life as new experience and new knowledge unfolds. I have always kept an open mind, a flexibility that must go hand in hand with every form of the intelligent search for truth.

### *Malcolm X*

When you find your definitions in God, you find the very purpose for which you were created. Put your hand into God's hand, know His absolutes, and demonstrate His love, present His truth, and the message of redemption and transformation will take hold.

### *Ravi Zacharias*

The Bible is one of the greatest blessings bestowed by God on the children of men. It has God for its author; salvation for its end, and truth without any mixture for its matter. It is all pure.

### *John Locke*

Always tell the truth - it's the easiest thing to remember.

### David Mamet

In wartime, truth is so precious that she should always be attended by a bodyguard of lies.

### Winston Churchill

A lie can travel half way around the world while the truth is putting on its shoes.

### Charles Spurgeon

Belief is a wise wager. Granted that faith cannot be proved, what harm will come to you if you gamble on its truth and it proves false? If you gain, you gain all; if you lose, you lose nothing. Wager, then, without hesitation, that He exists.

### Blaise Pascal

The Lord Jesus Christ did not come to Earth to make bad men good, the Lord Jesus Christ came to Earth to make dead men live.

### Ravi Zacharias

What lies are you living with? Ask Jesus Christ for the truth.

### Derek Rodgers

*__Psalm 96:13__*

*__For He is coming, for He is coming to judge the earth. He shall judge the world with righteousness, And the people with His truth.__*